The President & Eve of Retirement

THE PRESIDENT
&
EVE OF RETIREMENT

Thomas Bernhard

Translated by Gitta Honegger

Performing Arts Journal Publications
New York

© 1982 Copyright by Performing Arts Journal Publications
© 1982 Translations copyright by Gitta Honegger

First edition
All rights reserved
No part of this publication may be reproduced or transmitted in any form or by any means, electronic or mechanical, including photocopy, recording, or any information storage retrieval system now known or to be invented, without permission in writing from the publishers, except by a reviewer who wishes to quote brief passages in connection with a review written for inclusion in a magazine, newspaper, or broadcast.

Library of Congress Cataloging in Publication Data
The President and Eve of Retirement by Thomas Bernhard
Library of Congress Catalog Card No.: 82-80615
ISBN: 0-933826-24-9
ISBN: 0-933826-25-7 (paper)

CAUTION: Professionals and amateurs are hereby warned that *Eve of Retirement* and *The President* are fully protected under the Copyright Laws of the United States and all other countries of the Copyright Union. All rights, including professional, amateur, motion picture, recitation, lecturing, public readings, radio and television broadcasting, are strictly reserved. No performances or readings of these works may be given without the express authorization of the author or his agent. For performance rights, contact Kurt Bernheim, 792 Columbus Avenue, New York, N.Y. 10025.

Design: Gautam Dasgupta

Printed in the United States of America

Publication of this book has been made possible in part by grants from the National Endowment for the Arts, Washington, D.C., a federal agency, and the New York State Council on the Arts.

CONTENTS

THE THEATRE OF THOMAS BERNHARD   9

THE PRESIDENT   17

EVE OF RETIREMENT   115

SELECTIONS FROM THOMAS BERNHARD   209

    Is It A Comedy? Is It A Tragedy?   210

    An Actor   215

PAJ PLAYSCRIPT SERIES

General Editors: Bonnie Marranca and Gautam Dasgupta

OTHER TITLES IN THE SERIES:

THEATRE OF THE RIDICULOUS/Kenneth Bernard, Charles Ludlam, Ronald Tavel

ANIMATIONS: A TRILOGY FOR MABOU MINES/Lee Breuer

THE RED ROBINS/Kenneth Koch

THE WOMEN'S PROJECT/Penelope Gilliatt, Lavonne Mueller, Rose Leiman Goldemberg, Joyce Aaron-Luna Tarlo, Kathleen Collins, Joan Schenkar, Phyllis Purscell

WORDPLAYS: NEW AMERICAN DRAMA/Maria Irene Fornes, Ronald Tavel, Jean-Claude van Itallie, Richard Nelson, William Hauptman, John Wellman

BEELZEBUB SONATA/Stanislaw I. Witkiewicz

DIVISION STREET AND OTHER PLAYS/Steve Tesich

TABLE SETTINGS/James Lapine

ACKNOWLEDGEMENTS

I wish to thank Gertrude Kothanek from the Austrian Institute whose initial encouragement and active support helped get the entire Bernhard project started; Bonnie Marranca and Gautam Dasgupta for their interest in "difficult" writers before they become fashionable; Dr. Wolfgang Kraus, Dr. Thomas Nowotny; Liviu Ciulei and the cast of the American premiere of *Eve of Retirement*: Kathy Burns, Donald Madden and Betty Miller; Michael Earley for his editorial and dramaturgical assistance; Dr. Siegfried Unseld for taking chances; Sophie Wilkins, the inspired translator of Bernhard's novels for her advice and untiring moral support, and Thomas Bernhard, for his trust.

G.H.

THE THEATRE OF THOMAS BERNHARD

Gitta Honegger

"Men are so necessarily mad that not to be mad would amount to another madness"

Pascal

During the twenty years of his distinguished career as poet, novelist and playwright, Thomas Bernhard has become famous as a so-called "serious," i.e., "difficult" writer, heir to Kafka and kin to Beckett, whose highly theatricalized personal vision describes a moribund world. His bleak outlook, and secluded life in a tiny Austrian village at the foot of the Alps, have earned him the epithets "Alpine Beckett" and "Mountain Kafka"—tongue-in-cheek references to his literary status as well as his inaccessibility in both literary and life styles. As was the case with Kafka, it took a long time before Bernhard's essentially comic spirit was recognized. It is not a pleasant one, to be sure, but rather a mad laughter: the author's laughter, audible through the text, echoing from the typewriter, and from the wings, at the madness of the world. The laughter suggests his survival technique, the technique of The Fool who knows that all human existence in the face of history and of nature (which always means death) is madness. But instead of succumbing to the particularly German malaise of taking himself too seriously and becoming a pitifully pathetic figure (as Bernhard demonstrates with many of his stage figures), the author-as-The Fool ultimately defies madness by exaggerating, i.e., "performing," "staging" madness, in the process making a fool of everyone—the world, the characers and himself.

The threat of madness, inherent in the tension between a profound fascination with death and a defiant lust for life haunts the baroque sensibility which is epitomized in the architecture of Salzburg, the city Bernhard grew up in and learned to hate very early. He describes—or rather exorcises—his relationship to Salzburg in his four-volume autobiography about his youth: *Die Ursache, Der Keller, Der Atem, Die Kaelte (The Cause, The Cellar, Breath, The Cold).*

The performer's outrageous game with death found its perfect Austrian incarnation in the popular eighteenth century-figure of Augustin, a bagpipe player during the great plague in Vienna, immortalized in the song "Oh Du lieber Augustin, alles ist hin" ("Oh my dearest Augustin, everything's dead"). One night, while playing in a pub and distracting his huge audience from the ever present reality of death he got so drunk that on his way home he fell into a ditch where the plague victims had been dumped. He fell asleep on top of the corpses singing his famous song—and survived.

The Fool performing on a pile of corpses could stand as the Austrian artist's coat-of-arms. He can be found in the old market-place theatre and the street performers, resurfacing in the comic temperament of Viennese playwright Johannes Nestroy, and finally, coming to full bloom during the early twentieth century in the charismatic personality of Karl Kraus, Viennese critic, satirist, poet, editor, and catalyst in the breakthrough of the most innovative intellectual and artistic ideas fermenting in the ominously lethal political climate of his day.

This is Bernhard's spiritual ancestry. But his obsession with death is not just a fashionable Central European pose. It has very concrete roots in his personal history. Born in 1931 he was old enough consciously to witness the war. As an adolescent he was close to death several times in an embittered, often grotesque, four-year battle with tuberculosis and the stupidities of doctors.

Eventually, when he finds his voice, not as the opera singer as he had originally intended, but as a writer, he develops a language that represents the death of its culture. It is a language after death, a language of relics (i.e., quotes) reconstituting a culture, society as artifice. Although radically different in his approach, fellow Austrian Peter Handke shares a similar experience of language as a cultural prison no one can escape from.

> The words we speak really no longer exist. . . . The whole instrumentation of words that we use no longer exists. Still, it is not possible to fall utterly silent.
>
> <div align="right">(<i>Gargoyles</i>)</div>

Vera in *Eve of Retirement* continually quotes her dead father while she prepares for the celebration of Himmler's birthday, which she and her brother, a Chief Justice and former concentration camp commander, had been observing every year since the end of the war. Their language reveals how truisms, platitudes, and sayings have been passed on through generations and perverted to the point that they can be made to justify even the worst horrors. The First Lady in *The President* endlessly quotes her close friend the chaplain in all moral and philosophical matters. The chaplain in turn seems to derive his commonplaces from the "great French classics" which he abuses in his quotes. The President himself says about his wife:

> and she parrots whatever he says
> she doesn't understand what he says
> but she parrots it
> if the chaplain says dogs are innocent creatures
> she parrots it

In Bernhard's play *Immanuel Kant,* a (twentieth century) character named Immanuel Kant is on an ocean liner en route to New York to receive an honorary doctorate from Columbia University. He is accompanied by his parrot who can recite all the crucial lectures of the famous philosopher. (It turns out that he is welcomed in New York not by Professors of Columbia University but by doctors and nurses of "one of New York's mental institutions.")

Bernhard's method of quoting suggests a language structure that is cut off from its origin to exclude any possibility of expressing spontaneous, original thought. He has been criticized for being repetitious. But his is a conscious technique defining language as a system of quotations. If we don't quote others we quote ourselves. As soon as we speak, we are impersonators—of those closest to us, of those before us and, finally, of ourselves. Taken to the extreme this is, of course, madness: "I am speaking of myself only in quotation marks, as you know, everything I said is only in quotation marks," explains the mad prince in *Gargoyles* to his visiting doctor.

Bernhard's prose creates even more radically the feeling of a complete absence of origin, of truth. Usually one person is trying to retrace the life of another who is dead and in most cases has killed himself. The "narrator," in many of his novels a witness to the death of the person, or rather, to certain stages in his life which may or may not have led to his death, compiles notes—his own, those of the dead person—letters and information from third parties which frequently quote the person in question. In the process, the narrator often absorbs and begins to speak the language of the person he has studied as various texts, just like an actor. The theatre, then, which is based on the quoting, reciting, and impersonating of a text is to Bernhard more than a metaphor for human existence: it is the perfect sign for its mechanism.

"Everything begins with reproduction"
Jacques Derrida

Once in a television interview Bernhard talked about his method:

> In my books everything is *artificial,* that is to say, all characters, events, incidents take place on a stage and this *theatrical space (Buehnenraum)* is completely dark. Figures entering a *theatrical space,* a *theatrical* square are perceived more distinctly in their contours than if they were to appear in natural light, as is the case with the usual prose writing we know. In darkness everything becomes more distinct. And this is true not only for physical appearances, for the visual—it is the same with language. One has to imagine the pages in my book as *completely dark:* the word lights up, this is how it becomes *distinct* and *overly distinct.* . . . If one opens my books . . . one should imagine being in a theatre opening the curtain, with the first page the title appears, total darkness—slowly words emerge from the background, from the dark, gradually they transform into processes, external and internal ones, which manifest themselves all the more clearly precisely because of their artificiality.

The description evokes Freud's mystical writing pad as a model for the psychic mechanism of retaining memories, particularly in Derrida's reading of it in his "Freud and the Scene of Writing." In that essay, which is based on his translation of the German *"Darstellung,"* Derrida shifts the emphasis fron the more general "representation" to the very specific "staging" of dream contents, as a form of pre-conscious writing through which memory imprints its traces on the human mind. In *The Hunting Party* the General says of the Writer.

> You see he scribbles
> all over the walls of his mind
> all over
> a mind covered with writing
> a completely covered
> and therefore completely blackened
> mind
> scribbled on with such speed
> that already one line is scribbled right over the other
> like a madman
> The entire surface of his mind
> which he himself can't make out anymore

If Bernhard conceives all his writing in terms of theatrical performance, the stage—the actual playing area—is the human brain and its writing, usually the voice of one character in a manic attempt to backtrack, to decipher the traces of memory in the psychic mechanism:

> I always write about interior landscapes only, which most people don't see, because they can't see anything inside, because they always think if it's inside, it must be dark. In my books I never described an actual landscape.

From his essentially theatrical model for writing it seems a small step actually to use the stage as the physical playing area. But whether his plays take place in a German town, or on an ocean liner, in a Portuguese resort or an Austrian hunting lodge, they are always explorations of the dark, interior landscapes of the mind where the language is Ariadne's thread guiding and protecting the speakers from getting lost, from death. Yet every word establishes death, dead matter only: quotes, memories, the past relived again and again, the same ambitions, fears, needs endlessly enacted in the frantic effort to erase and kill them, which is also the only way to keep them alive, that is to say, to keep their speakers alive.

Perhaps it is no coincidence that Bernhard's final paper for the Salzburg Mozarteum, where he graduated in acting and directing, took Artaud as its subject. Although they arrive at diametrically opposed conclusions, Artaud and Bernhard share a profound disgust and fascination with the theatre as the most openly decadent model of representation as death. But while Artaud's dusgust leads him to the vision of a new theatre without repetitions (rehearsals), Bernhard accepts no way out of the confinement within language. His plays embrace language in a macabre dance of death, exposing its limitations and its traps, and revelling in this exposure, illustrating it from all possible angles, vomiting the words, and repeating them to death. Yet the end result is not the destruction of language but a fascinating deconstruction of our inherited repertoire of idioms, a language structure haunted by genius and guilt and fossilized in cliches which empahsize the artificiality not only of theatre but of all conversation as reproductions, compositions of ready-mades, dead objects:

> As soon as we look at a person
> very carefully
> we see
> that he is dead
> one existence after the other
> and what we hear
> is something already dead
> What we are told
> what we must practice and study
> at all times
>
> (The Writer in *The Hunting Party*)

Derrida outlines human existence as *representation* which is both death and death deferred. Bernhard's dramaturgy offers a perfect model for this paradox. His plays always juxtapose one character's monological mania with another's silence. The latter is the stimulant, the catalyst and mirror, the resistant surface which absorbs the traces and fissures of the spoken word that assure the speaker of his existence.

In *Eve of Retirement* Vera and Rudolf speak incessantly. Is it to reinforce their past, to justify their pathetic existence or to exorcise it? Or is it to kill their memories? The ambiguity their relationship reflects culminates in one of the most chillingly hilarious scenes in contemporary dramatic literature as the characters look through the family photo album where snapshots of concentration camps and war incidents alternate with idyllic childhood pictures.

"We photograph things in order to drive them out of our minds. My stories are a way of shutting my eyes" says Kafka.

Among Bernhard's twelve major plays, *The President* and *Eve Of Retirement* are his most popular ones. [*Eve of Retirement,* which had its 1981 American premiere at the Guthrie Theatre in Minneapolis under Liviu Ciulei's direction, is also Bernhard's most frequently produced play in Germany.] This may be because these are his most accessible plays. Presumably, they are more accessible because they deal with recognizable political themes: *Eve Of Retirement* features a family of contemporary Nazis, *The President* deals with the dictator of a small country which is shaken by anarchist revolts and assassinations. Nazism/Fascism and terrorism: a neat link is established. A major European author deals with his culture's past and present. The plays take place in familiar landscapes.

But the obvious message is just the surface, as such thin ice, which a careful reading will quickly prove. It might even (mis)lead us to a quick concemnation of the thin ice, which we must either leave immediately or break through the surface to end up where Bernhard's plays really take place: in the darkness of the human mind. This is the setting for Freud's "scene of writing" which Derrida calls "the stage of history and the play of the world." Each character carries his own theatre inside his head. Like a puppet he is attached to the strings of his language which keeps him in motion. There are no periods, no commas, because any punctuation mark would create a caesura and the strings would be cut and the puppets collapse.

> "He went on to speak of the admiration for a person that we generate in ourselves. Suddenly that person can brutally destroy that admiration by suddenly becoming, in our very presence, and simultaneously inside us, the very thing he constantly and in reality is."
>
> Thomas Bernhard in *Gargoyles*

How does a translator meet an author after having lived or imagined to have lived inside his head for so long? I feel I know the man. I took possession of his world, I slipped inside his language, I made it my home. Now that I sit across from him, in his secluded farm house, everything seems somewhat ridiculous and slightly perverted. I feel like a voyeur who had spent years peeking through his window, and watching him do all sorts of things, with his knowledge. But he doesn't know exactly what I've seen. I hope he doesn't bring up the subject. I hope he doesn't want to talk about his work. I don't want to talk about it. We wouldn't talk about the same thing anyway. What he has written belongs to him. What I have read belongs to me. Is there a point of contact that hasn't yet been explored by myth, gossip, research, scholarly comment, by my own imagination?

I know the myth, the gossip:

He is a recluse. Unpredictable. Inaccessible. Strange. No one gets close to him and those who do or say they did, are cut off suddenly. He publicly attacks Austria's most sacred institutions. And not without malice: the man who has achieved the status of a classic master of twentieth century literature writes letters to newspapers in the tone of a naughty, mischievous schoolboy.

I know his biography:

He was born in Holland in 1931. Both his mother and father were Austrian. Descendants of farmers, peasants, horse-dealers, innkeepers, butchers from Salzburg and Upper Austria. He never knew his father. The closest and most influential person in his life was his grandfather, Austrian novelist Johannes Freumbichler, whose work was rediscovered only recently, posthumously. The grandfather taught the adolescent boy music, literature, philosophy and the unavoidable necessity to live alone. He inspired many of Bernhard's characters: people obsessed by one idea to help them get through their loneliness, which, on the other hand, drives them deeper and deeper into isolation, eventually madness, and finally death. By the age of seventeen he becomes ill with what doctors diagnose as tuberculosis. He is committed to a sanitarium where he eventually finds out that he didn't have tuberculosis but was infected with it during his stay in the ward for terminal cases.

His first published work is poetry and very lyrical, musical theatre pieces. His breakthrough as a novelist comes in 1963 with his first novel *Frost*. Since that time he has been living—for the most part alone, but with frequent intervals of escape-like sojourns in other countries—in the farm house in Upper Austria where I now visit him.

I feel extremely self-conscious. I don't know the man sitting across from me. He is intruding in the world I had created around "my" author. I am intruding in his home. After he had offered me a seat on a wooden bench next to a beautiful old tiled stove he sits down in the opposite corner of the ascetically furnished room. I feel on stage. "What are you looking at?" he asks me after he had looked at me long enough to make me feel uncomfortable while I tried not to. "Nothing," I say, with the stupid grin I was afraid of. "That's impossible," he replies, explaining to me patiently how one can never look at *nothing,* how one is always looking at *something.* I try to come up with a profound answer. But I can't pick up a proper cue. He had stopped talking. "Why are you giving me this funny look?" he finally asks.

Suddenly I catch the glint in his eyes. The face, in an instant, becomes familiar: it belongs to the voice I've known all along. Behind these eyes I recognize The Fool waiting in ambush. "Because I can't make any sense out of this!" A pause. Then he laughs: "Actually, you are right. Come to think of it, I can't either." The visit, finally, is not about "meeting the author." It is an encounter with yet another of his texts.

The photographs which I didn't take would show:

The monastic facade of the old restored farm house in an Andrew Wyeth landscape; interiors of white surfaces and clean angles emphasized by wooden beams; a flight of doors framing more interiors of white surfaces, straight lines and right angles; no pictures, no superfluities; selected pieces of beautiful rustic furniture. Images of displacement: the Mercedes in the rectangular farm yard behind the awesome wooden gate; the antiseptic stainless steel surfaces of the ultra-modern kitchen appliances; the electric clock on the wall behind the rough wooden table framing the timeless silence that belongs to the house.

Surfaces and silences.

A tall, graying country squire in the traditional pose of Hapsburg chivalry: kissing his female visitor's hand. The gesture, because it is authentic, seems anachronistic. The most intangible surface: his aura of serenity suggesting a gentleness preserved in aloofness and repeatedly glossed over by how I remember him best: the ancient features of The Fool.

On my way back to the train station I pass a bookstore in the village. His latest autobiographical work *Die Kaelte (The Cold)* has just come out. It is prominently displayed. I buy the book and finish reading it before the train arrives in Vienna. I feel tremendously happy: the visit had not violated the truth of his fiction.

THE PRESIDENT

Characters

President
First Lady
Colonel
Actress
Mrs. Frolick
Masseur
Maid
Waiter
Ambassador
2 Funeral Attendants

Officers
Members of the Administration
Diplomats
People

Place

The first, second and fifth scenes take place in the Presidential Palace. The third and fourth scenes take place in Estoril, Portugal.

Scene 1

That period of humiliation was followed by centuries of cruelty and anarchy . . . every citizen became either murderer or the murdered one, hangman or the hanged one, oppressor or the oppressed, in the name of God or in search of the Savior. . . .

Voltaire

Bedroom, nine a.m.
Two dressing tables.
Next to the right dressing table a basket for a dog, which is empty.
Two clothes racks, chairs, easy chairs.
The door to the bathroom is open.
Splashing of water in the tub.
The First Lady in her negligee at the right dressing table.
Mrs. Frolick enters, dressed in black, carrying a pile of black clothes for the President, who is in the bathroom; she deposits the clothes on the chair next to the left clothes rack, hangs a top hat on the clothes rack and exits again.

FIRST LADY: (*Looking after her.*)
　Ambition
　hate
　that's all
　(*Mrs. Frolick enters with a pile of black clothes for the First Lady, which she deposits on the chair next to the right clothes rack, she hangs a black veil on the clothes rack.*
　First Lady jumping up, grabbing the black dress.)
　The Chanel
　the Chanel
　(*Holds the dress up to her body, looks into the mirror.*)
　It's gone out of style
　it's out of style Mrs. Frolick
　(*Throws the dress on the floor, commanding Mrs. Frolick.*)
　Pick it up
　Up up
　(*Mrs. Frolick picks up the dress.*
　First Lady looks at the veil.)
　It's out of style
　No more Chanels Mrs. Frolick
　(*Looks at the empty basket.*)

Not the Chanel
(Splashing in the bathtub.
The President coughs.
Mrs. Frolick and First Lady look at the bathroom door.)
MRS. FROLICK:
But it's your favorite dress madam
FIRST LADY:
It could have been a shot through the head
(Takes the dress away from Mrs. Frolick.)
He could have been shot through the head
a shot through the President's head
from an ambush
fatal
a shot through the head Mrs. Frolick
(Pressing the dress against her body.)
It's my favorite dress
but it's out of style
A shot through the head
through the head Mrs. Frolick
I bought it in Paris
My son was with me
(Presses the dress even closer to her body.)
On Rue Campon
The House of Chanel Mrs. Frolick
For my brother's funeral
his uncle's funeral
three years ago
Carmen had just opened
My husband's favorite opera
(Looks at the bathroom door.)
The anarchists
are everywhere
Mrs. Frolick
Nothing will stop them
nothing Mrs. Frolick
(Throws the dress on the floor.)
They are proceeding
very systematically now
The chaplain says
that they are lunatics
They hate my husband Mrs. Frolick
Did you read what they wrote
The President must go
they said
the President must go
(Splashing in the bathtub.)

This country has never had
such a President
such a good President Mrs. Frolick
This country never had
a better President
than my husband
(*Mrs. Frolick picks up the dress.*)
It's completely out of style
Bring me the Halston
(*Mrs. Frolick hesitates.*)
Go ahead
What are you waiting for
go ahead
(*Mrs. Frolick exits with the black dress.
First Lady calling after her.*)
The Halston
Mrs. Frolick
If the bell rings
it should be the new colonel
(*To herself.*)
A tragedy
what a tragedy
(*Calls out.*)
And don't forget the towels
And let the masseur in
But only if he's got a pass
only with a pass Mrs. Frolick
(*Splashing in the bathtub.
First Lady sits down, looks in the mirror.*)
A shot through the head
He could have been shot through the head
We should never have gone to the Unknown Soldier's Memorial
(*Calls into the bathroom.*)
Not to the Unknown Soldier's Memorial you hear
(*Splashing in the bathtub.*)
They'll get you some day
(*Looks in the mirror.*)
It wasn't him
It wasn't our son
(*Calls into the bathroom.*)
Is the wound still bleeding
If your would's still bleeding
(*Splashing in the bathrub.*)
It's only natural
that our son
should join

the anarchists
(*Calls into the bathroom.*)
The new colonel has worked
on your funeral speech
you hear
something short for the old colonel
(*To herself.*)
Not to the Unknown Soldier's Memorial
The chaplain told us years ago
that suddenly one day
he'd join the anarchists
(*Sticks out her tongue, to herself, into the mirror.*)
After the funeral
you'll lock yourself up
and work on your part
you understand
you will be acting
the way you always did
(*Calls into the bathroom.*)
The tickets for the Christmas show
have been sent out already
four hundred and fifty tickets
A benefit
for the retarded
(*Looks in the mirror.*)
It wasn't him
They're after the brains
the chaplain says
the ones
who have power
you have power
you hear
power
(*Looks in the mirror.*)
Power
(*Takes a comb from a drawer and starts combing her hair.*)
My child
in Rome
(*Calls into the bathroom.*)
Abroad
you hear
studying archaeology
(*Looks in the mirror, sticks out her tongue, then:*)
Excavations
Ancient objects
Works of art

Skeletons
(*Sticks out her tongue, then:*)
He just left
in the middle of the night
without a word
without anything
He joined the anarchists
(*Calls into the bathroom.*)
There is no proof
that he's actually joined the anarchists
(*Looking in the mirror.*)
An archaeologist
A natural scientist
and archaeologist
(*Splashing in the bathtub.*)
In the dead of night
without a word
gone
Leaving everything
behind
(*Throws down the comb.
Calls into the bathroom.*)
how can he shoot at us
if he's in Rome
remember
that's where we bought him
his Tacitus
(*Looks in the mirror.*)
Schliemann
(*Combs her hair again.*)
My child
(*Calls into the bathroom.*)
That's where he met
that writer
and suddenly he was completely
captivated by that man
I never trusted
that man
(*Looks in the mirror.*)
Right here
from behind the bushes
at the Unknown Soldier's Memorial
while he is in Rome
(*Throws down the comb, looks in the mirror.*)
The intellectuals
exploit the talents of the inexperienced

the chaplain says
they incite them
even against their own parents
(*Mrs. Frolick brings in the Halston dress.*)
Not a day without a funeral
Eight funerals in two weeks
Mrs. Frolick
(*Masseur enters behind Mrs. Frolick and stands there, waiting.
First Lady to Masseur.*)
My husband is waiting for you
go on in
(*Masseur quickly bows to the First Lady and goes into the bathroom.
First Lady to Mrs. Frolick.*)
Let me see
Give it to me
(*Inspects the dress.*)
Did you
take it in
Put it down
there on that chair
there
(*Mrs. Frolick puts the dress on the chair.*)
did you
take it in
on both sides
(*Pulls at the hem.*)
You have to pull the hem
pull the hem Mrs. Frolick
pull
very gently
pull
pull
(*Suddenly.*)
Is your son
also an anarchist
listen Mrs. Frolick
is he an anarchist
go on tell me
if your son
is an anarchist
go on tell me
(*Hands her the dress.
Mrs. Frolick very carefully puts the dress on the chair.*)
Just a bunch of kids
with nothing but destruction
in their heads

keeping us in constant fear
fear
you understand
(*After a pause.*)
One day I'll have caught up with you
then my face will be
as gray and old
as yours
But you've had your gray old face
for twenty years
You haven't changed
in all those years
Time passes unnoticed
if one is born with such a face
it leaves no marks
on such a gray old face
Soon I'll have caught up with you
It won't take long now Mrs. Frolick
Now they strike out
now they destroy us
Soon both of our faces
will be equally gray
The colonel had to die
because they missed my husband
Had they not missed my husband
had the colonel gotten away
but the colonel is dead
The colonel gets a state funeral
all flags are half staff
Mrs. Frolick
He'll get a cannon salute
(*Mrs. Frolick exits.*
First Lady calling after her.)
Your son has always been
very intelligent
Mrs. Frolick
(*Looks in the mirror.*
Splashing in the bathtub.
First Lady puts make up on her left eye lid.)
There
(*Puts make up on her right eye lid.*)
There
You wake up
you get up
you become the First Lady
First Lady

(Combs her hair.)
The First Lady
Soon our faces will be
equally gray
(Puts on make up.)
You take on the part
of First Lady
(Moaning and groaning of the President from the bathroom. First Lady talking toward the bathroom.)
My husband
went into shock
into shock
The third assassination attempt
within four weeks
But he loves
to go to the Unknown Soldier's Memorial
(Looks in the mirror.)
First Lady
(Leans back and bursts out laughing.)
First Lady
(Suddenly she stops laughing and looks at the empty basket.)
you see
(Puts on make up.)
Some red
some gray
Some black
some more red
Some gray
Every day we do the same
my darling
We get up
We wash up
We get dressed
Then breakfast
(Looks at the empty basket.)
Some more red
some more black
(Looks at the empty basket.)
We made a mistake
We shouldn't have gone
to the Unknown Soldier's Memorial
Those horrible people
And then you get
what you've been asking for
right
(Puts on make up, combs her hair.)

What we've been asking for
PRESIDENT: (*From the bathroom.*)
　　Who are you talking to
FIRST LADY: (*As if looking for something under the dressing table.*)
　　To him
　　to him
　　(*To the empty basket.*)
　　To you
PRESIDENT: (*To the Masseur.*)
　　She's talking to the dog
　　you hear
　　my wife
　　is talking to her dog
　　who's dead
　　That's good
　　Aaahh
　　(*Laughs.*)
FIRST LADY: (*Looking at the empty basket.*)
　　Crazy
　　Some more red
　　Some black
　　(*Looking at the empty basket.*)
　　Killing
　　killing
　　an innocent creature
　　(*With her face close to the mirror.*)
　　Killing
　　an innocent creature
　　(*Looks at the empty basket.*)
　　You
　　(*Looks in the mirror, suddenly:*)
　　If it was him
　　(*Looks at the bathroom door.*)
　　our son
　　(*Mrs. Frolick enters with several towels for the President.*)
　　Anything new
　　did the papers bring
　　anything new
　　about the assassination
　　They didn't catch them
　　they didn't get them
　　not yet
　　A Secret Service
　　that is unable
　　to protect the President
　　(*President coughs.*

First Lady calling suddenly into the bathroom.)
Go away
you must go away for a few weeks
(Mrs. Frolick back from the bathroom.)
How's the weather report
Mrs. Frolick
(Mrs. Frolick wants to say something.)
No
Nothing new
it stays the same
gray
gloomy
(Looks in the mirror.)
Funerals
There's an anarchist in everyone
Mrs. Frolick
Your son
is a suspect
Mrs. Frolick
(Mrs. Frolick exits.
First Lady looking after her.)
A suspect
(Looks in the mirror.)
As if all we're left with
are enemies
(President coughs.)
Every mind
is an anarchistic mind
the chaplain says
every head an anarchist's head
(President coughs.)
If it was him
It wasn't him
(Combs her hair.
Mrs. Frolick enters with a pair of black shoes, which she puts down near the dressing table.)
There is no proof
Not one single proof
Mrs. Frolick
(Mrs. Frolick exits.
First Lady to herself.)
I saw
his face
very clearly
behind the bushes
in my dream

(*Powders her face.
Calls toward the bathroom.*)
Our son an anarchist
ridiculous
(*Mrs. Frolick brings in a pair of black stockings.
She helps the First Lady into the left stocking.*)
Under surveillance
Because we've spoiled him
Mrs. Frolick
Because he's had everything
Because we let him dominate us
But he isn't degenerate
the chaplain says
(*Sticks out her left leg to make it easier for Mrs. Frolich to put on her black stocking.*)
His face Mrs. Frolick
very clearly
again and again
his face
and the Unknown Soldier's Memorial
And then the shot
Imagine
my husband were dead
Mrs. Frolick
(*Mrs. Frolick helps the First Lady into her right stocking. First Lady sticks out her right leg to make it easier for Mrs. Frolick to put on her right stocking.*)
Our son an anarchist
ridiculous
Because for years we've had
all sorts of dark chaotic minds
passing through our house
Here you'd always meet the most dangerous brains
(*Looks at the empty basket.*)
If it was him
but it wasn't him
(*President coughs.
First Lady to Mrs. Frolick.*)
Would you comb my hair
(*Mrs. Frolick combs her hair.
First Lady looks at the empty basket.*)
Poor little dog
What's that poor dog got to do
with it all
Anarchists are lunatics
the chaplain says
(*Calls toward the bathroom.*)

What kind of body guards are they
Some kind of body guards
(*Pulls back her right leg.*
Mrs. Frolick gets up.
First Lady looks at the empty basket.)
And you
poor little dog
And I
who was so used to you
Seventeen years
that poor little thing's been
lying in this basket
my little darling
my little pet
The anarchists
take everything
Shooting
to kill
from an ambush
suddenly
Mrs. Frolick
(*President coughs.*
First Lady to the empty basket:)
To kill
you
(*Looking in the mirror.*)
Some kind of police
who can't even deal with those criminals
(*Sudden noise from the shower in the bathroom.*)
Killers
(*To Mrs. Frolick's face.*)
Killers
killers
(*Mrs. Frolick exits.*
First Lady looking at the empty basket.)
Because you had
such a weak heart
(*President coughs.*
First Lady to the mirror.)
What a mess
(*Very close to the mirror.*)
A mess
A mess
(*Mrs. Frolick enters with a large picture of the dog.*)
Put it over here
(*Points to the dressing table.*)

Right here
(Mrs. Frolick puts the picture on the dressing table.
First Lady looks in the empty basket, picks up the picture.)
What a beautiful animal
Those eyes
Mrs. Frolick
They shot him
brutally
from an ambush
(Turns toward Mrs. Frolick.)
The bullet
the second bullet Mrs. Frolick
was meant for me
Why should that dog have to suffer
(Notices that Mrs. Frolick is dressed in black.)
Black
You are wearing black
Mrs. Frolick
Take off that dress
immediately
not you Mrs. Frolick
No black for you
You have no right
to wear black
take off that dress immediately
(President coughs.)
You have no right
(Mrs. Frolick exits.
First Lady calling after her.)
Not you Mrs. Frolick
(Looks in the mirror.)
I am wearing black
We are wearing black
Not you
PRESIDENT:
  No no
  the colonel didn't suffer
  the first shot killed him
  on the spot
MASSEUR:
  And now your other side
  Mr. President
  this way
  you see Mr. President
FIRST LADY:
  The colonel didn't suffer

    I am going
    going
    going
    to the mountains
    to the Alps
PRESIDENT: (*To the Masseur.*)
    My wife is going
    to the Alps
    I'm also going away for a few days
    to Portugal
    to Estoril
FIRST LADY: (*Looking at the empty basket.*)
    Who knows
    what's going on
    in those anarchists' heads
    Killing an innocent life
    (*Full of disgust.*)
    Just killing it
    (*President coughs.*
    First Lady combs her hair, looks in the mirror.)
    Right after the funeral
    I'll start working on the play
    with the chaplain
PRESIDENT: (*To the Masseur.*)
    My wife accepted
    the lead
    in the chaplain's Christmas show
    She's seriously interested
    in the art of acting
    The play will take her mind
    off the assassination
    It will also help
    to distract her
    in this gloomy time of year
FIRST LADY: (*Staring at herself in the mirror.*)
    Am I afraid
    afraid
    (*Sticks out her tongue.*)
    Help
    help
    (*Looks at the empty basket.*)
    What we love
    is taken from us
    shot
    murdered

PRESIDENT: (*To the Masseur.*)
   Lunatics
   a bunch of lunatics
   In her dream my wife saw
   our son
   shooting at us
   imagine
   our own son
   at us
   from an ambush
   such a sensitive boy
FIRST LADY: (*Hears what her husband is saying.*)
   Such a sensitive boy
PRESIDENT:
   Such a brilliant mind
FIRST LADY:
   Such a brilliant mind
   (*Suddenly screaming toward the bathroom.*)
   The basket's got to go
   (*Looks at the empty basket.*)
   The basket's got to go
   I can't look at that basket anymore
   I don't want the basket here
   (*Mrs. Frolick enters in a red dress.
   First Lady to her:*)
   The basket's got to go
   take it out
   it must go
   take the basket out
   out
   go
   go
   (*Mrs. Frolick wants to take the basket.*)
   No don't
   don't
   don't take it out
   I am crazy
   crazy
   Leave the basket
   leave it here
   here
   don't take it out
   (*Mrs. Frolick leaves the basket where it is.*)
   As long as the basket's still here
   (*Suddenly to Mrs. Frolick.*)

Make his bed
make his little bed
his little bed you hear
fluff it
fluff it
(*Mrs. Frolick busies herself with the empty basket.*
First Lady staring at her activities.)
Fluff it
fluff it up
(*President coughs.*
First Lady to Mrs. Frolick.)
Fluff it every day
fluff his bedding
every day
fluff it every single day you hear
soft and puffy
Mrs. Frolick
his pillows soft and puffy
fluff those pillows
Mrs. Frolick
(*Mrs. Frolick shakes out the pillows.*)
There
now
(*Mrs. Frolick steps back.*
President coughs.)
Light
light and fluffy
That's how he liked it
light
soft
light Mrs. Frolick
(*Gestures to Mrs. Frolick that she can leave.*
Mrs. Frolick wants to leave.)
No
stay right here
I see a wrinkle
(*Points to the basket.*)
one tiny wrinkle
one last wrinkle Mrs. Frolick
(*Mrs. Frolick smoothes out the wrinkle in the bedding.*)
Nice and smooth
it must be nice and smooth
He likes it nice and smooth
(*Mrs. Frolick gets up, wants to leave.*
First Lady to her face.)

Don't ever mention him
again
never again
not one word
ever
(*President coughs.*
First Lady looks at the bathroom door, then:)
Not a word
you just make his little bed
but don't say a word
not one word
We'll keep the basket right here
you understand
we'll fluff it
we'll keep it
(*Notices suddenly that Mrs. Frolick is wearing a red dress.*)
Red
A red dress
(*Laughs.*)
A red dress
(*To Mrs. Frolick's face.*)
Outrageous
(*Puts on more make up.*
Mrs. Frolick exits.
President coughs.)
Nobody understands
they don't understand
(*Referring to Mrs. Frolick.*)
These sort of people
understand nothing
but spite
ambition
hate
that's all
(*Looks at the empty basket.*)
I can see you
(*Bends down to the empty basket.*)
I sure do
my little darling
(*Suddenly softly.*)
We'll stay together
forever
you understand
forever
(*Gets up and straightens out the dog's blanket.*)

There
that's the way
(*Sits down at the dressing table only to look right back at the basket.*)
You and the colonel
They'll crack down hard
on those anarchists now
(*President coughs.*)
they'll crack down hard
(*President and Masseur laugh out loudly.*
First Lady looks at the bathroom door.)
crack down hard
(*President and Masseur laugh.*)
They'll have to pay for it
(*Mrs. Frolick enters with a pile of mail and puts it on the dressing table.*)
Have all these letters
been properly checked
have they been opened
Mrs. Frolick
did you open and check them
all of them
The anarchists are mailing
explosive letters Mrs. Frolick
If you receive and open such a letter
you'll have your hands blown off
or your whole body might blow up
Mrs. Frolick
(*Staring at the letters, questioning.*)
Every single letter

MRS. FROLICK:
Every single letter

FIRST LADY:
All the mail

MRS. FROLICK:
All the mail
(*President amd Masseur laugh out loudly.*
First Lady and Mrs. Frolick look at the bathroom door.)

FIRST LADY:
In all secrecy
while he's massaging my husband
the masseur is telling him
jokes
jokes
(*President and Masseur laugh out loudly.*
First Lady takes a letter.)
A man like my husband

expects to be killed
at any moment
(*President and Masseur laugh out loudly.*)
That man
has been massaging my husband
for twenty-one years
The masseur was here
even before you
(*Throws the letter away.*)
Hypocrisy
nothing but hypocrisy Mrs. Frolick
(*Takes another letter and throws it away.*)
The Finance Minister
who wheedled his way into office
and then exploited my husband
(*Takes a third letter, reads it.*)
People keep writing about poverty
yet they don't even know
what poverty is
I know what poverty is
my husband also knows
The President also knows
what poverty is
(*President and Masseur laugh out loudly.
First Lady throws the letter away.*)
We know
what poverty is
My husband
has worked his way up
from the bottom Mrs. Frolick
all these letters
begging for money
belong in the garbage
(*Takes a fourth letter, reads it.
President laughs.*)
The colonel's wife
begging for her sons
she wants to send all five of them
to the Military Academy
(*Puts the letter on the dressing table. Suddenly to Mrs. Frolick.*)
Where did you put the black crepe
Did you iron his crepe
(*Mrs. Frolick leaves, returns with a long strip of black crepe.*)
My husband could never
appear at those funerals

without the crepe
(*Mrs. Frolick puts the crepe over the back of the left chair and stands there.*)
Half an inch
and the President
would've been dead
no doubt
comb my hair
(*Mrs. Frolick combs her hair.*)
There we stand
and stare at the ground
and we feel nothing
because we stand there so often
and stare
then suddenly
it's someone close to us
Death completes
life
the chaplain says
(*Looks at the empty basket.*)
Should we bury
or burn him
burn
or bury him
(*Calling suddenly toward the bathroom.*)
Watch
that the blood doesn't rise to his head
Sir

MASSEUR:
    I am massaging
    our Mr. President's
    very gently
    Our Mr. President's head
    isn't bleeding anymore

FIRST LADY:
    Isn't bleeding anymore

MASSEUR:
    Only a very gentle massage

FIRST LADY: (*Her head almost touching the dressing table.*)
    You see
    in this position
    with my head
    almost touching the table
    I can feel the pain
    (*Sits up again.*)
    That comes

from standing for so many hours
at so many graves
with my head always down
(*Mrs. Frolick massages the First Lady's head and shoulders.*)
Very gently
down the neck
into the shoulders Mrs. Frolick
My son
hates his father
If we don't exercise the head
it will perish
the chaplain says
He is a renegade Mrs. Frolick
on the brink of
excommunication
First it was the Interior Minister
then the Foreign Minister
then it was the Chancellor
then the press secretary
then the correspondent for the *Corriere della Sera*
Then let me think
the executive director
of the State Opera
finally they shot Merz the bank president
and after Merz Honsig
and after Honsig Taus
and after Muellner Helmreich
and after Friedrich Wallner
and after Wallner Peter
They killed nineteen people
before the colonel Mrs. Frolick
Tell me
just before the colonel
(*President coughs.*
President and Masseur laugh out loudly.)
Who was shot before the colonel
Two days before the colonel
they shot the head of the transit system
The head of the transit system
(*Looks at the empty basket.*)
And you
my darling
Things have been leading up to this
for many years
the chaplain says

it started at the universities
they are the seed beds Mrs. Frolick
Suddenly several hundred students
were put under arrest
then again a few hundred
they rallied against us
Mrs. Frolick
they demonstrated at the Presidential Palace
you're hurting me
watch it
A demonstration
at the Presidential Palace
(*Points to the window.*)
From this window
I saw them coming
Hundreds at first
then thousands
tens of thousands Mrs. Frolick
Then there was violence
violence
And our son
was among the arrested
The chaplain talked to him
He went to America
we put him on a plane
to the United States
then after only six weeks
back to Europe again
He was seen in Paris
(*President and Masseur laugh out loudly.*)
Then off to Rome
After all he is an archaeologist Mrs. Frolick
He is writing a book
he is smarter than his teacher
already today he has far
surpassed his teacher
in the field of archaeology
(*Looks at the empty basket, then to the window.*)
The masses
the masses marched
toward the palace
From behind the curtain I watched
the masses march on the Palace
They hurled rocks through our windows
Many have been executed Mrs. Frolick

executed
Then there was peace
For a long time there was peace
but a year ago
they started again
they aren't marching anymore Mrs. Frolick
now they blow up buildings
and they kill important people
people who are most important to our country
experts leaders in their field
Mrs. Frolick
in cold blood
It will take a while the chaplain says
before the President strikes back
(*Looks at the bathroom door.*)
Once again my husband will strike
(*Mrs. Frolick combs the First Lady's hair.*)
and when he does
he does it without mercy
Mrs. Frolick
Then there'll be hundreds of executions
every day Mrs. Frolick
Those hoodlums
destroying our beautiful country
destroying it willfully
willfully Mrs. Frolick
willfully
(*Looks at the empty basket.*)
who even kill an innocent life
Killers
butchers
But maybe
the terrorists will quiet down
no they won't
The chaplain says
that things will get much worse
There'll be more terror and worse atrocities
more and worse Mrs. Frolick
more misery
worse fears
Aren't you afraid of the terrorists
of some anarchist trying to get you
You open a book because you want to read
and you are blown into pieces
aren't you afraid

everybody
everybody
The whole country is ruled by fear
The Church tries to pacify
it wants to pacify
but it can't
the Church has lost touch
with everyone
on either side
the Church is parasitical
parasitical Mrs. Frolick
I know all about the Church
The chaplain hides nothing from me
The Church itself is ruled by chaos Mrs. Frolick
Corruption
ambition
hate
that's all
(*Looks at the black clothes.*)
How long have we been wearing nothing
but black
But you haven't lost any relatives yet
not one
You have no business mourning Mrs. Frolick
outrageous really your outfit
but actually it suits you well
quite well
Red very pretty
Red and long
(*Looks at her ankles.*)
down to your ankles
red
If I didn't know
that this was once my dress
mine Mrs. Frolick
just think
that I once wore this long red dress
I wore it a lot
if I didn't know this
I'd have to think you're taking some quite offensive
liberties
showing up like this
red from top to bottom
outrageous
revolting

but it was I who gave you that dress
I forced it on you
literally forced it on you say didn't I
force you
order you to put it on
And you did
With great pain no doubt
with the most excruciating pain
You were quite young then
You didn't yet have your gray complexion
Your face has been gray for twenty years
so I must have given you that dress twenty years ago
Do you remember
how I forced you
I just pulled it out of the closet
and threw it on the floor
(*Points to the floor.*)
Right there Mrs. Frolick
You see
And you picked it up
and put it on
without contradiction
(*President and Masseur laugh out loudly.*)
To tell you the truth my husband is scared
very scared Mrs. Frolick
but he doesn't show it
while we show our fear
you are scared too
although you know
you have no reason to be scared
he doesn't show it
of course he needs his distractions
his regular massages for example
his pacing the Palace
that's how he gets his best ideas
or reading Metternich
his one and only Metternich
Metternich
Metternich Mrs. Frolick
or he plays chess with the colonel
(*Laughs.*)
With the colonel
The colonel doesn't suffer anymore
(*To Mrs. Frolick, confidentially.*)
Believe me

the colonel's death hit him the hardest
the two were inseparable
not only at the chess board
not only at the chess board
Time takes from us
what we love most Mrs. Frolick
those who survive
have their hearts torn out
(*Looks at the empty basket.*)
brutally
mercilessly
After the funeral
right after the funeral
before I start learning my lines
I'll drop by
at the coroner's lab
(*Looks at the empty basket.*)
I want to see him one more time
Then I'll have to decide
whether to burn
or bury him
(*Looks at Mrs. Frolick's face.*)
What would you say
say something
why don't you say something
(*Mrs. Frolick takes a step back.*)
You are torturing me
all you do
is torture me
the only goal of people like you
is torturing others
every one of your kind has found someone
he can torture
You are torturing me
why don't you say something
go on say something
say something
Mrs. Frolick
This is an order
(*Looks at the empty basket.*)
I'll have him burnt
burnt
(*To Mrs. Frolick's face.*)
I have to see him one last time
You hated that dog

You always hated him
deeply Mrs. Frolick
very deeply
most deeply
and you know why
you were jealous
and now
that he's dead
that the poor thing's dead and gone
you still hate him
Such hate
Ambition
hate
that's all
When you fed him
you hated him
When you walked him
you hated him
hated him
when you fixed his leash
you hated him
when you made his bed
you hated always hated him
Ambition
hate
that's all
(*President and Masseur laugh out loudly.*)
My husband also
hated that dog
But it was a different kind of hate
different
from your hate
And now that he's dead
he pays no more attention to him
He is amazed
that I still talk to him
(*Looks at the empty basket.*)
I got into the habit
of talking to myself
I got it from him
but I'm not talking to myself Mrs. Frolick
I'm talking to him
I talk to him about everything
I always asked him first
Whatever I had to do

I always asked him
first
my first recourse
(*Looks at the empty basket.*)
I did nothing
without asking him
a tragedy Mrs. Frolick
My husband always asked the colonel
I asked him
my husband had his colonel
I had him
the colonel was my husband's first recourse
(*Looks at the empty basket.*)
My first and my last recourse
was my dog
(*Looks at the bathroom door.*)
And now we've lost both
to a terrorist's bullet
(*To Mrs. Frolick's face.*)
I saw his eyes and knew
that he was dead
Heart failure Mrs. Frolick
heart failure
The dog suffered a heart attack
from the shot that killed the colonel
Those gaping questioning eyes Mrs. Frolick
and I threw him away
just threw him away
I dropped him Mrs. Frolick
and he fell to the ground
(*Looks in the mirror.*)
I didn't understand
My husband was long gone
The terrorists
the anarchists were gone
I stood there alone
bent over him
But my husband had to go to the Unknown Soldier's Memorial
he took a walk there every day
with me
with the two of us
Don't ever walk the same route twice
the chaplain says
not twice
every day

at the same time
we didn't realize the danger
When he
my husband
noticed the bluejay on top of the Unknown Soldier's Memorial
he raised his cane
to point at the bluejay
he raised his cane Mrs. Frolick
that saved his life
had he not raised his cane against the Unknown Soldier's Memorial
he would have been the victim
this way the colonel was the victim
A matter of seconds Mrs. Frolick
a matter of seconds
And the second shot up in the air
the anarchists probably got scared
since their first shot missed the President
(*Looks at the empty basket.*)
Your son
is a suspect
Mrs. Frolick
(*To Mrs. Frolick's face.*)
Your son is enrolled
at the university isn't he
isn't he Mrs. Frolick
(*President and Masseur laugh out loudly.*)
A country
in fear Mrs. Frolick
(*Looks at the bathroom door.*)
Ambition
hate
that's all

Curtain.

Scene 2

First Lady with veiled face sitting at the dressing table. Mrs. Frolick behind her.

FIRST LADY:
    I can see
    but no one can see me
    I can see everything
    I can see myself
    myself Mrs. Frolick
    in the mirror
    me
    I can see you too
    standing right behind me with always the same
    gray face
    Soon I'll have caught up with you
    Then we'll be equal Mrs. Frolick
    (*Turns toward the bathroom door.*
    President and Masseur laugh out loudly.)
    That laugh
    I've always found it repulsive
    (*To herself.*)
    Like everything else about that man
    everything
    repulsive
    You understand Mrs. Frolick
    everything
    because I hated him
    because he repelled me
    Ambition
    hate
    that's all
    It's him the anarchists are after
    but they could never get him

not yet
you hear Mrs. Frolick
(*President and Masseur laugh out loudly.*)
Not yet
And then what
Then I'll be the President's widow
I ask myself
who will be next
will it be the Minister of Justice
or the Foreign Minister
could it be our new Foreign Minister
or perhaps our new Interior Minister
Soon this country will have lost
its last sound and able head
not one brilliant extraordinary mind
the chaplain says
you hear Mrs. Frolick
The Archbishop has given up his strolls
through his palace gardens
he no longer leaves his room
he's too scared
everybody is scared
scared everybody you hear
at first no one was scared
But now even the clergy are scared
The Archbishop may be next
The anarchists have their own special strategy
And if we liquidate one faction Mrs. Frolick
another one is ready to move
until they've reached their goal
(*To Mrs. Frolick's face.*)
Your son is a suspect
Philosophy students
are the most dangerous
the chaplain says
and theologists
philosophy and theology
are the real poison
poisoning this country
murdering our nation
by murdering us
(*President and Masseur laugh out loudly.*)
We had much too much
freedom
the chaplain says

loosen the reins
and you'll have anarchy Mrs. Frolick
(*Looks in the mirror, her face almost touching the mirror.*)
I can see
but no one can see me Mrs. Frolick
Those artists
whom I always supported
painters sculptors
poets Mrs. Frolick
musicians
they know no gratitude
Patronizing the arts
is utter nonsense
All artists need a kick in the ass
the chaplain says
In the ass
all those artists and their art
right in the ass Mrs. Frolick
(*After a pause.*)
This is how
my portrait should've been painted
just like that
Just like that Mrs Frolick
(*Pulls the veil off her head.*)
not like that
(*Throws the veil on the floor.*
President laughs out loudly.
First lady ordering Mrs. Frolick around.)
Pick it up
pick up the veil
up up
(*Mrs. Frolick picks up the veil.*)
You take the veil
you take it
(*Mrs. Frolick puts on the veil.*
First Lady laughs out loudly, then shouting suddenly:)
you have no right
to wear that veil
you have no right
no right
take off that veil
take it off
off
(*Mrs. Frolick takes off the veil.*)
You must show your real face Mrs. Frolick

(*Points to the clothes rack.*)
There
hang up that veil right over there
(*Mrs. Frolick hangs up the veil on the clothes rack.
First Lady looks at the bathroom door.*)
What a laugh
That this man
always has to laugh
he always laughs
(*Looks at the empty basket.*)
we hated him
he hated us
Ambition
hate
that's all
(*Mrs. Frolick combs her hair.*)
The way you smell
is the kind of smell
that reminds me of poverty
but the way you breathe
is reassuring
regular and reassuring
then again quite irregular
quick short breaths
and I don't know
what's going on inside you
controlling the mind controlling the body
the chaplain says
Physical discipline
mental discipline
as a way of life
you understand
(*Pathetically.*)
I adore
the chaplain's mental discipline
The heads of the Church
are anarchists' heads
the chaplain says
My husband mistrusts
the Church
To be born with a head
that never stops thinking
the chaplain says
to be stuck with a head
that always dissects everything

He is a renegade
on the brink of
excommunication
When I first met him
I felt nothing but dislike for him
although I admired
his mastery of French
The way he read Zola to me Flaubert
(*Looks at the empty basket.*)
even he was spellbound
that perceptive little creature
sitting next to me
and Goethe you hear
Marcel Proust
and finally Voltaire
Voltaire
Voltaire
When he
Voltaire
met his donkey at the gate
to his country estate in Ferney Mrs. Frolick
meeting his donkey at the gate
he'd say
Please after you Mr. President
(*Mrs. Frolick laughs out loudly.*
First Lady shouts at her.)
Be quiet
you have no right
to laugh about this
Not you
Please
said Voltaire to his donkey
when he met him at the gate
after you Mr. President
The chaplain's pronunciation
especially when he reads Voltaire
superb
superb
He refused a chair at the Sorbonne
for my sake Mrs. Frolick
(*Mrs. Frolick massages the First Lady's neck.*)
I can feel the warmth
rising gently
to my head
according to medical law

very gently
(*Suddenly, referring to the chaplain.*)
Imagine
at the age of three
he'd been abandoned by his mother
abandoned
abandoned
Put in a hammock
on a fishing boat
with foster parents
in Rotterdam
His mother subjected him
to abject poverty
but only those people
who come from the gutter
make it way up to the top
Poverty breeds superior minds
Such a gruesome childhood Mrs. Frolick
blossoming into genius
Marcel Proust as the chaplain says
is a genius
The worst childhood
is the greatest asset Mrs. Frolick
He said that too
He says something significant
at least once a day
But if he never writes down
what he says
it will all be lost
It's history's loss
Mrs. Frolick
if the chaplain won't write it all down
At some later date he says
he will write down
what he considers important enough
to write down
at some later date
That date hasn't come
And I make every effort
to take notes
of everything he says
but I keep losing my notes
True genius the chaplain says
works its way up from the bottom
And Pascal says

to be that is enough
(*Suddenly commanding Mrs. Frolick.*)
Now the legs
massage my legs
(*Sticks out her right leg.*
Mrs. Frolick massages her right leg.)
It takes a man who has seen the world
a man like the chaplain
who knows all continents
all continents Mrs. Frolick
to be able to come up
with such significant thoughts
All outer and all inner
continents
Every outside
every inside
knowing your outer as well as your inner
geography
and using your mind like a surgeon's knife
you understand
Giving up a chair at the Sorbonne
to read Zola to me
and Flaubert
and Marcel Proust
My husband hates him
He also knows history
better than anyone
it's not a waste of money to employ
such an outstanding mind
(*Looks at the empty basket.*)
And how he loved him
More than anything
He always brought him something
Even roast beef
even roast beef Mrs. Frolick
peanuts
bananas
sandwiches Mrs. Frolick
sandwiches
once he fed him
piece by piece
(*Sticks out her left leg.*
Mrs. Frolick massages her left leg.)
every one of the twelve sandwiches
the most delicious sandwiches

I ever made
he put them
one by one into his little mouth
(*Looks at the empty basket.*)
it was music Mrs. Frolick
a symphony
amazing
What the chaplain says about Pascal
applies to himself as well
His own thoughts
have the quality of the *Pensees*
But why do I talk to you about this
I talk to you
and you don't understand
what I am talking about
(*President and Masseur laugh out loudly.*)
How much security
and yet what insecurity
comes from a genius
a thinking mind such as the chaplain's
is reassuring on the one hand
unsettling on the other
That is the source of all inspiration
(*Pulls back her left leg.*)
And this type of man even has style
How some people
or heads as he would say
can pick any subject
and understand it right away
(*President and Masseur laugh out loudly.*)
I've considered
cutting
all funding for the arts
because artists are the seedbeds of anarchy
as my husband says
and the chaplain would agree
but I won't cut those grants
The artists' grants
will not be cut
Where did you put the speech
the new colonel prepared for my husband
(*Mrs. Frolick exits and returns with the speech.
First Lady takes it, reads:*)
We must seek retribution for this crime
as we mourn here

at the open grave
A good friend
a loyal citizen
(*To Mrs. Frolick.*)
Isn't it grotesque
that the new colonel has to write
the eulogy for his predecessor
not without tragic overtones Mrs. Frolick
(*Reads aloud.*)
standing at the open grave
of this truly selfless man
this courageous officer
in the service of our country
our country
our country
our country
(*Puts the speech on the dressing table, sticks out her tongue.*)
our country
(*To Mrs. Frolick.*)
When you give my husband his cough syrup
give me some too
remember
two spoonfuls for my husband
two spoonfuls for myself
perhaps it will help me
memorize my part
in the children's show
As you know I've been playing the lead
for twenty years
reluctantly in the last few years
quite reluctantly
but they keep after me
and I keep playing
I wonder
if it is proper for me
to appear on a stage
in a time like this
in such tragic times
in a time of so much misery
What would you say
That I appear on stage
while we are going through such awful times
That I perform in a play
right after returning from yet another funeral
from yet another grave of a dear murdered man

It is difficult for me
to stand at an open grave Mrs. Frolick
As I'm standing there
I see myself not at an open grave
but on a proscenium stage
saying my lines
those funny lines from a children's show Mrs. Frolick
and I ask myself
how long before I forget myself
It could happen quite easily
that suddenly
instead of standing there in speechless sorrow
I start saying my lines
those funny lines Mrs. Frolick
those funny lines
(*President and Masseur laugh out loudly.*)
I ask myself
why did I initiate you
into the secret of a good massage
(*Mrs. Frolick massages the First Lady's neck again.*)
From the center moving outward
Always think of drainage
Massaging the germs
out of my body
The thoughts
the images that come to me
while you're massaging me
And I wonder
what do you see
what do you think
when I'm massaging you
So much that laid buried
gets released suddenly
(*President and Masseur laugh out loudly.*)
Of course you
don't have to be scared
The anarchists
won't touch you
yet it could happen
by mistake
by mistake
if by mistake you
(*Looks at the empty basket.*)
As he was shot
Dead

When I think how he propped his head
on the rim of the basket
That faithful little creature
would watch me for hours
reading Flaubert
or Zola
or Camus you understand
the great French writers
who always fascinated me
the most
What's going on
inside
such an innocent creature
We'll never know
He took his secret with him
to the grave
(*Looks at the bathroom door.*)
They wanted to kill him
He's the one
they had in mind
(*Looks at the empty basket.*)
Instead they killed
that poor little dog
The chaplain says
they are lunatics
young people
who got trapped
inside their own heads
Mrs. Frolick
It's the intellectuals
(*President laughs out loudly.*)
My husband
is scared too
but he doesn't show it
he can't afford to show
his fear
I can show it
both of us can
and how
(*To Mrs. Frolick's face.*)
And how you show your fear
for which you have no reason
You don't have to be scared
I do
You don't

Everything I am
predisposes me to fear
the chaplain says
while there's nothing about you
that warrants
even the slightest fear
(*To her face.*)
Only by mistake
Mrs. Frolick
My stockings are loose
(*Sticks out her right leg, Mrs. Frolick adjusts her stocking; sticks out her left leg, Mrs. Frolick adjusts her left stocking.*)
That the anarchists could rob me
of my greatest treasure
But the world doesn't understand
They don't want to understand
they can't understand
(*Mrs. Frolick gets up, after the First Lady has pulled back her legs.*)
All those eulogies
the colonel had to write
before his death
not exactly flawless speeches Mrs. Frolick
not without style
but not his own
He could have written his own eulogy
his own eulogy Mrs. Frolick
(*Takes the speech from the dressing table, reads:*)
And now we shall lower
this loyal man
into our native soil
those of us assembled here
in mourning
may ask
what did this loyal servant of our country
sacrifice his life for
but we know for what
he sacrificed himself
(*Throws the speech on the dressing table to Mrs. Frolick.*)
Do you know for what
the colonel sacrificed himself
Do you know
I am asking you
do you know
he sacrificed himself you hear
the colonel sacrificed

himself
(*Looks at the bathroom door.*
President laughs.)
For the last few years
they've been thinking only
of how they could eliminate him
(*Suddenly loudly.*)
They can't be treated like humans
those anarchists
not like humans
up against the wall
the nearest wall
the chaplain says
On the other hand
(*Looking for something.*)
Where did I put my pin
the long hair pin Mrs. Frolick
(*President runs the shower.*)
The pin
Mrs. Frolick
(*Mrs. Frolick bends down to look for the pin.*)
The chaplain is all for putting them
against the wall
On the other hand
on the other
But the chaplain is not the Church
(*President coughs.*
Mrs. Frolick has found the pin, gets up.
First Lady sticks the pin in her mouth.
Mrs. Frolick takes the pin out of her mouth.)
You are right
keep reminding me
of my bad habit
such a bad habit
such a common but nonetheless bad habit
putting a pin in my mouth
(*Straight to Mrs. Frolick's face.*)
what a bad habit
Immediately after the funeral
I must attend to
my family business
remind me Mrs. Frolick
(*Mrs. Frolick wants to say something.*)
Don't say anything
I must see

my business manager
and the coroner
(*Looks in the empty basket.*)
and study my part
my lines
in the children's show
all at once
(*Suddenly.*)
Where is the colonel lying in state
MRS. FROLICK:
In the old armory
FIRST LADY:
The old armory
and from there
a procession
to the National Cemetery
MRS. FROLICK:
The National Cemetery
FIRST LADY:
This will be one great demonstration
against anarchism Mrs. Frolick
the chaplain says
PRESIDENT: (*To the Masseur.*)
Give me a good rub
a good rub
good
that's it
(*Laughs.*)
FIRST LADY:
If you own a business
as large as the one
I've brought into my marriage
exactly the size it is now
you can't always keep your eye
on everything
not always Mrs. Frolick
Fluctuations in the market
retirements
promotions
and the thefts Mrs. Frolick
(*Mrs. Frolick bends down.*
First Lady looks to the floor.)
It must be there
there
there

(*Mrs. Frolick gets up with the pin.*)
Now don't put it in your mouth
not in your mouth
A business such as ours
naturally tempts people to steal
If you'd know how many employees
have been caught red-handed Mrs. Frolick
Sometimes we only find out after years
But we always find out
We always catch those thieves
(*Looks at the empty basket.*)
You
my dearest
what have you got to do with it
(*To Mrs. Frolick.*)
Make sure they don't burn
his choker too
You must bring me his choker
His beautiful choker
the choker
with the gold buttons
(*To the empty basket.*)
They robbed me of you
They robbed me
those anarchists
of you
(*To Mrs. Frolick.*)
Did you hear me
The choker
and be careful
when you take it off
(*With her head bent.*)
I was horrified
by what I saw
at some coroner's inquests
(*To Mrs. Frolick's face.*)
Imagine
they brought both
the colonel
(*Looks at the empty basket.*)
and him
to the coroner
(*President comes out of the bathroom, the Masseur behind him.*)
FIRST LADY: (*Suddenly, very ostentatiously, to make sure that everyone can see what she is doing, grabs Mrs. Frolick by the wrist, squeezing it hard. To her husband:*)

What would I do without her
(*Lets go of Mrs. Frolick's wrist.*
President wears nothing but a towel wrapped around his belly.
Mrs. Frolick approaching the President with a pair of long johns.)
MASSEUR: (*Bowing to the President.*)
Thank you Mr. President
goodbye Mr. President
(*Bowing to the First Lady.*)
Goodbye madam
(*Exits.*)
PRESIDENT: (*Calling after him, while Mrs. Frolick helps him into his long johns.*)
Don't forget
to bring the lemon balm tomorrow
The lemon balm
(*President sits down at his dressing table.*)
FIRST LADY: (*To Mrs. Frolick.*)
Show my husband
the speech
(*Takes the eulogy from her dressing table, hands it to Mrs. Frolick, who hands it to the President.*)
Pretty good style
I think
the writing of your new colonel
your new protector
your aide
only the old buddies
who qualify for retirement
are assigned to you
to the President
PRESIDENT: (*Reading through the speech.*)
I hope my new colonel's duties
won't be limited
to composing eulogies
(*Mrs. Frolick helps the President first into his right, then his left, sock, while he is reading the speech.*)
FIRST LADY:
Mrs. Frolick has ironed your black crepe
Is your wound still bleeding
(*President touches his head.*
First Lady gets up and goes to him.)
Your wound stopped bleeding
A grazing shot
barely a grazing shot
(*Kisses his forehead.*
Points to the speech.)

There
you see
Retribution he says
we must seek retribution
(*Laughs out loudly, returns to her dressing table, sits down.*)
Retribution
is a stupid choice
of expression
the chaplain says

PRESIDENT: (*After Mrs. Frolick has finished putting on his socks.*)
Circumstances didn't permit me
to pursue my favorite subject
natural science
my son pursues
no
no no

FIRST LADY:
Why didn't you tell Mrs. Frolick
that in nineteen thirty four
you had the choice between two
ambassadorial posts
she isn't interested
not anymore
just as I am no longer interested
Because you arrived at the capital
at the crucial moment
and took charge of everything
(*Mrs. Frolick combs the President's wet hair.*)
A chance meeting
an influential person
after the disastrous outcome of the war
(*Imitates her husband.*)
Then I began
to immerse myself in Metternich
reading nothing but Metternich
About dynasties
About the Slavic Nation etcetera
About dual powers
About creatures with two heads
one of which is always
the more active part etcetera
About caesuras in history
Identity etcetera
I am all for letting people say
what they want to say

as long as they let us do
what we want to do etcetera
always cautious
always pessimistic
(*To Mrs. Frolick.*)
Do you hear my husband
he's always saying the same thing
I hear what he says
I always hear what he says
for thirty years I've been hearing
the same thing over and over again
Ruling nations
Dual nations
Concessions
and then
The most fateful of all deeds etcetera
And then
toward four in the afternoon
while he's pretending
to converse with me
about our chancellor
(*Mrs. Frolick helps the President into his T-shirt, then his shirt, she brushes his cut away while he buttons up his shirt.*
First Lady putting on make-up, looking in the mirror.)
Soon they'll have shot
the last sound and able head

PRESIDENT:
The new colonel
is an excellent officer

FIRST LADY:
Just like the old colonel
who was unable
to protect you
He should've warned you
He should've told you to stay away
from the Unknown Soldier's Memorial
Because he should've known
that the anarchists
would strike again
(*Looking in the empty basket.*)
Soon they'll have killed
the last sound and able head
the chaplain says
(*Looks to the window.*)
Looking out

and always in fear
(*Looking in the mirror.*)
This is the last time
I am performing in a children's show
Suddenly my mind goes blank
I don't remember a word
there I stand
unable to say a word
Silence
and the other actors stare at me

PRESIDENT:
I always liked you
in that children's show
You didn't develop
your talent
You could've become a great actress
No kidding
(*Mrs. Frolick helping the President into his cutaway pants.*)
I've always been attracted
to women
who can act
women who love Shakespeare
Moliere
I only like opera
(*Explains.*)
Spectacles

FIRST LADY:
Where are you meeting her

PRESIDENT:
In Madrid

FIRST LADY:
In Madrid
Why make it so complicated
and wait till Madrid
why not just take her with you

PRESIDENT:
Gossip my dear
no gossip now
(*Sticks out his right leg for Mrs. Frolick, who puts on his right shoe.*)
No gossip now
(*Sticks out his left leg.*
Mrs. Frolick puts on his left shoe.)
She's already in Madrid
If I didn't have the funeral
I'd be there too by now

an elegant city
(*To Mrs. Frolick.*)
You should go there
and buy yourself a pair of shoes
You get the most elegant shoes in Madrid
and in Lisbon
(*Mrs. Frolick adjusts the President's shirt.
President to Mrs. Frolick.*)
You are still wearing
the shoes
of your late mother
Mrs. Frolick
(*Looks at her shoes.*)
They are completely out of style
Go there
go to Madrid
FIRST LADY: (*Looking in the mirror.*)
One more time
then never again
never
the last time
my last appearance on a stage
the last time
on stage
(*Looking at the empty basket.*)
But once you get involved
in this sort of thing
you can't get out anymore
PRESIDENT:
Did you know
that the play originally
was the Archbishop's idea
The first draft
was by the Archbishop
FIRST LADY: (*Looking at the empty basket.*)
My poor little critic
my poor little darling
You always watched me
practicing my part
in front of the mirror
you watched
and listened
he had such a good ear
(*To the President.*)
and I could tell immediately

if I did something wrong
My tone of voice
my facial expression
This kind of part
is purely psychological
the chaplain says
(*Looks at the empty basket.*)
Because you had such a weak heart
The anarchists
killed you
Our national enemies
If they'd gotten him
No they had to get you
the colonel and
because of your weak heart
you
Ambition
hate
that's all
(*To Mrs. Frolick.*)
Be careful
when you bandage his head
careful

PRESIDENT:
Very careful
Mrs. Frolick

FIRST LADY:
Dead on the spot
One shot
and he was dead
Poor little thing
I didn't even see
that the colonel was hit
I thought
the dog's been hit
Heart failure
(*Looks at the empty basket.*)
my darling
right in my arms
(*Turns around and demonstrates.*)
this is how
I dropped him
just like that
on the ground
the dog is dead

I thought
  and I dropped him
  (*To Mrs. Frolick.*)
  You understand
  just dropped him
  dead as he was
  lifeless
  (*Demonstrates the whole scene once again.*)
  This way
  just like that
  (*Looks in the mirror again.*)
  He was still warm
  We got off with our fright
MAID: (*Entering.*)
  The colonel
FIRST LADY:
  Show the colonel in
  (*Looks at her watch.*)
  Almost ten
  (*Maid exits.*)
  When is the funeral Mrs. Frolick
MRS. FROLICK:
  At eleven
  madam
PRESIDENT:
  All funerals are
  at eleven
  All state funerals
  (*Colonel enters with a briefcase, bows to the First Lady, then to the President.*)
  Come on in colonel
  come on in
FIRST LADY: (*To the Colonel.*)
  Have you caught the assassins
COLONEL:
  No madam
FIRST LADY:
  No
  no
PRESIDENT:
  Not yet
  (*President indicates to the Colonel to show him the files.*)
COLONEL:
  Pardons
  Mr. President
  Three pardons

> The chancellor has already signed them

FIRST LADY:
> The chancellor has signed them
> the chancellor has signed them
> but the President won't sign them
> my husband won't sign
> (*Vehemently, to the President.*)
> No more pardons
> no more pardons
> (*Mrs. Frolick with the black dress in front of the First Lady.*)
> No more pardons
> Who are those people

COLONEL: (*While going through the files with the President.*)
> So called lifers
> Madam
> so called lifers

FIRST LADY:
> Meaning serious cases

COLONEL:
> Very serious cases

FIRST LADY:
> I've always loathed
> those Christmas pardons
> Come November
> we are swamped with petitions for clemency
> (*To the President.*)
> Don't you dare sign
> No one gets pardoned
> No more pardons
> (*Colonel closes his files.*)
> This is not the time
> to pardon anyone
> no more mercy
> no more mercy
> (*To Mrs. Frolick.*)
> Why are you standing there
> help me into my dress
> (*Mrs. Frolick helps the First Lady into her dress.*
> *First Lady keeps talking.*)
> I always loathed those pardons
> Not now
> not now
> (*Into the mirror.*)
> Never
> (*Has gotten into her dress, turning to the President.*)

No more pardons
How dare you
(*Turns toward the empty basket, looks into it.*)
When I just lost
my greatest treasure
(*To the Colonel.*)
You may go now
Go
By the way
your speech is a masterpiece
the speech about your predecessor
a masterpiece
(*Colonel exits, bowing constantly.
First Lady calling after him.*)
A masterpiece
a masterpiece
(*To the basket.*)
a masterpiece
(*To the President.*)
Those pardons are an anachronism
an anachronism
an anachronism
(*Sticks out her right leg.
Mrs. Frolick puts on her right shoe.*)
An anachronism
(*Sticks out her left leg.
Mrs. Frolick puts on her left shoe.*)
We shouldn't have gone
to the Unknown Soldier's Memorial
(*Directly to the President.*)
Asking you to pardon
the most serious criminals
at a time like this
(*Looks at the basket.*)
is an obscenity
(*President slips the suspenders over his shoulders.*)
Because I suddenly
had the idea
to walk down
to the Unknown Soldier's Memorial
(*Looks out the window.*)
while I actually had planned
to go and buy myself
a new hat
(*To Mrs. Frolick.*)

Not a black hat Mrs. Frolick
don't think
a black hat
nothing black
Downtown
to the hat store
instead
I went to the President's office
(*To the President.*)
And I made you come to the park with us
to the Unknown Soldier's Memorial
(*Looks at the empty basket.*)
How happy that dog was
how he took off
immediately
and ran around the Memorial
Suddenly the shot
I threw my dog away
(*Demonstrates it.*)
that's how I threw him away
just like that

PRESIDENT:
The colonel
died
immediately
only twenty steps away from the spot
where the chancellor was killed
twenty years ago

FIRST LADY:
The time has come
where everything is upside down
the chaplain says
There is an anarchist
in everyone
Every head if it's a clear head
is an anarchistic head
Perhaps
the chaplain says
this is the revolution
(*To Mrs. Frolick.*)
Make sure to change my husband's sheets
they must be changed every day
He gets everything bloody
during the night
without his bandage

(*To the President.*)
Only a light scratch
on the head
so light
you can hardly see it
but
(*President files his fingernails, then puts cold cream on his face. Mrs. Frolick combs the First Lady.*)
You have watched me
with the butcher
You've seen everything
and suddenly you'll talk
you'll talk just at the right time
So far
But then
my husband knows about it
and to be perfectly honest
it was the chaplain's idea
If my husband can fool around all night
with a third rate actress
He knows what I am doing
we have no secrets
don't you dare give my husband
the slightest hint
How well you look in that dress
Like a child of the revolution
My cast off clothes
suit you well
You're wearing my old clothes so well
(*To the President.*)
Don't you think
she looks great
in my old clothes
(*To Mrs. Frolick.*)
Mrs. Frolick you're born
to blossom
in your masters' cast off clothes
What a vast difference
between the two of us
(*Looks at the empty basket, then:*)
No more dog
no dog
You have such delicate hands Mrs. Frolick
(*Suddenly grabbing Mrs. Frolick's hands, intentionally hurting her. President turns toward the two.*

First Lady lets go of Mrs. Frolick.)
Such harsh features
and such delicate hands
Like a lady
But there's something repulsive
about the way you comb my hair
the way you help me into my clothes
The way you come through the door
Every time you come in
I think
Why does she come in now
But you never explain
in twenty years
you've explained nothing
(Keeps picking up her jewelry and putting it back on the table again.)
You torture me
as I torture you
(Turns toward the President.)
and both of us are torturing him
You unconsciously
I do it consciously
according to a specific plan
And he tortures all of us
(Picks up the picture of the dog and puts it back down on her dressing table.)
all of us you understand
he has the power
to torture everybody
Everything is torture
ambition
hate
that's all
The chaplain says
it all comes down
to the absurdity
of human contact
PRESIDENT:
   The colonel
   will get a memorial
FIRST LADY:
   Usually reserved for artists
   poets composers
   world renowned artists
   (Sticks out her tongue.
   President coughs.)
   The streets

have been cordoned off
for the funeral procession
and there will be black flags
on all public buildings
And all schools will be closed
Mrs. Frolick
PRESIDENT:
By a hairsbreadth
FIRST LADY:
By a hairsbreadth
the President escaped his death
Theatrical
political
pathetic
(*To Mrs. Frolick.*)
I am exhausted
exhausted
The brutality of protocol
It isn't easy
being the President's wife
let alone the President
(*President picks up his collar from the floor and fastens it to his shirt.*)
Since the middle of October
we're wearing only black
and every other day the avenues
are blocked off for a state funeral
And soon they'll die by the hundreds
the chaplain says
the heads of both the Church
and the State
Because nature demands its dues
Harvest time
the chaplain says
harvest time
(*Rises in front of the mirror.*)
But I look great in black
great
just great
MRS. FROLICK:
Black looks good on you
madam
FIRST LADY:
You know exactly
what I want to hear
That's you

    always telling me
    what I want to hear
    always torturing me
    (*Grabs Mrs. Frolick's hand and holds it tightly.*)
    but I can't
    (*Lets go of Mrs. Frolick's hand.*)
    always be running around
    in mourning
PRESIDENT:
    The colonel was a fine man
    he told me he wants
    all his five sons
    at the Military Academy
FIRST LADY: (*Takes a theatre ticket from her dressing table.*)
    The Friends of Music
    still send me tickets
    to the Philharmonic
    The art of the fugue Mrs. Frolick
    Johann Sebastian Bach
    (*Gives the ticket to Mrs. Frolick.*)
    The proletarian woman
    sitting in the President's seat
    But don't lose the ticket
    One of your colleagues
    lost her ticket once
    (*Mrs. Frolick puts the ticket away.*)
    People come in
    from the country
    looking for stimulation
    but the city isn't stimulating
    it doesn't stimulate
    (*To the President.*)
    this city isn't stimulating
    (*To Mrs. Frolick.*)
    You can see
    how sad it is
    in our cities now
    And soon we'll have
    real anarchy
    the chaplain says
    Do you remember the time
    you combed
    me
    and the dog in turns
    at my command

PRESIDENT:
    There's a huge paper conspiracy
    against us
    all the newspapers
    every one of them
    a massive paper conspiracy
    (*Mrs. Frolick brushes the President's top hat.*)
FIRST LADY: (*Looking at the empty basket.*)
    Now I miss you so
    but your smell is still here
    I can smell you
    (*To Mrs. Frolick.*)
    Your arch enemy
    is dead
    dead
    (*Looks in the mirror.*)
    My voice is hoarse again
    The cough syrup
    the cough syrup
    (*To Mrs. Frolick.*)
    When you give my husband his cough syrup
    give me some too
    (*To the President.*)
    You get your sore throat
    from all those funeral speeches
    (*To herself, into the mirror.*)
    And then
    suddenly
    losing my lines
    Why all those children's shows
    but we are getting
    old
    and soft
    (*To the President.*)
    The proceeds go toward the purchase of wheelchairs
    the latest models
    (*From now on Mrs. Frolick slowly wraps the strip of black crepe around the President's head.*)
    from Germany
    The Germans make the most sophisticated
    wheelchairs
    Polio
    is coming back again
    and tuberculosis
    all of a sudden

(Picks up the picture of the dog and puts it back down on her dressing table.)
everyone
has tuberculosis
or polio
The sanitariums are overcrowded
Your actress
Miss Gerstner
I hear got a part
in a classical play
a small part that is
(Sticks out her tongue, puts a pearl necklace around her neck.)
Now is the time for comedy again
The days are getting gloomy
and the theatres play comedies
They should be prevented from playing comedies
at a time like this
Couldn't the colonel be put to rest
in peace and quiet
A state funeral
Because the state likes it that way
The chaplain says
there's nothing more embarrassing
than a state funeral
or any of those pompous funerals
staged by and for the VIP's
In peace and quiet
(Takes off her pearl necklace and puts it on her dresser.)
Soon I'll know
every cemetery in town
And all the speeches
The new colonel's speech
is just like the old colonel's speeches
Don't you think
the anarchists
should simply wait
just wait and see
because the ones they want to kill
are dying off all by themselves
dying off
dying off
(Holds the pearl necklace to her neck again.)
In droves
the political elite are dying off in droves
no need for violence
they are dying on their own

(*Puts down the pearl necklace for good.*
Mrs. Frolick has helped the President into his vest and jacket, he gets up, Mrs. Frolick brushes him off once more from top to bottom, puts the top hat on his head.)
PRESIDENT:
　Where is my speech
　Mrs. Frolick
　(*Mrs. Frolick hands him the speech, he puts the speech in his jacket.*)
FIRST LADY: (*Gets up after a glance at the empty basket.*)
　The VIP's
　are dying in droves
　they are dying on their own
　(*President and First Lady center stage.*
　Mrs. Frolick gets the veil from the clothes rack and puts it on the First Lady.
　President and First Lady embrace.
　A huge rock is hurled through the window.
　Everybody startled, standing still.)
COLONEL: (*Enters and says:*)
　The cortege is waiting
　Mr. President

Curtain.

Scene 3

Hotel Inglaterra.
President and Actress at a table, laughing.
Waiter enters and clears the table.
President and Actress laugh out loudly.

PRESIDENT: (*Wiping his mouth with his napkin.*)
    How you ran
    barefoot
    over hill and dale
    while the colonel was waiting for us
    worried
    that there might have been an accident
    Remember the bench
    next to the garden gnome
    where you played
    your new role for me
ACTRESS: (*Hitting the table top.*)
    I played
    my new role for you
PRESIDENT:
    To memorize it
    My feet
    you can't imagine
    my feet
    but I didn't take off my shoes
    not I
ACTRESS:
    If a man is always in boots
    and his feet aren't used to shoes
    his shoes will hurt him
    if he's chasing over hill and dale

PRESIDENT:
    Chasing you
    you
    my child
    chasing you
    (*President and Actress laugh out loudly.*
    Waiter, after putting several bottles of champagne on the table, opens one of them.)
PRESIDENT:
    Time my child
    can't be turned back
    (*Quotes from Voltaire.*)
    Nothing lasts longer
    than time
    for it is the measure
    of eternity
    Nothing is shorter
    for we lack it
    in all our endeavors
    nothing passes more slowly
    for the one who waits
    yet ever too fast
    for the one who enjoys
    (*Waiter pours more champagne, first for the Actress, then for the President.*)
    it can expand to infinite length
    but it can also be broken down
    to infinitesimal units
    everyone takes it for granted
    but regrets its loss
    nothing can happen without it
    through it anything unworthy of posterity
    will pass into oblivion
    (*With his head held up high.*)
    but it will grant immortality
    to that which is great
    (*To the Waiter.*)
    You can go now
    Leave us alone
    alone
    (*Waiter exits with the dishes.*
    President kisses the Actress on the cheek.)
    Then
    remember
    we went to Estoril
    on foot

The colonel immediately thought
that something had happened to us
people like him always think
that something must have happened
that's the way they are trained
The old colonel
fell in love with Oporto
the old buddy
The new one's never seen the Atlantic before
People like him who see
the Atlantic
for the first time
are completely overwhelmed
by that experience
(*Suddenly lifting the table cloth.*)
It's the same table
There
you see
it's the same table
(*Points to a certain spot on the table.*)
This is where I carved
something in the table
the last time we were here
Our initials
You were drunk my child
That's when I did it
as I was watching you
you had fallen asleep
you fell asleep my child
you were so tired
we had just returned from Sintra
that's when I carved
our initials in this table
it actually is
the same table
(*Drops the table cloth.*)
I told them
it had to be the same table
But they could have said
it was the same table
while it wasn't the same table
it is the same table
They have the best hotels
in all of Europe
The toughest tightest management

What luxury my child
What are we living for
if we can't enjoy
this kind of luxury
every now and then my child
a little luxury
with no one
bothering us
(*They both drink.*)
I requested
the same suite
and the same table
for our dinner
The initials prove
it is the same table
(*Calls toward the door.*)
Colonel
(*Colonel appears in the door.*)
Go to sleep
colonel
I won't need you anymore
we won't need you anymore
(*To the Actress.*)
Right my child
we won't need the colonel anymore
Good Night colonel
Tomorrow at nine at the President's
you hear
why don't you knock at seven thirty
you'll be amazed colonel
about protocol in Portugal
COLONEL: (*Bowing.*)
Good night Mr. President
(*Exits.*)
PRESIDENT:
And this is called
my bodyguard
my bodyguard
(*Actress laughs.*)
And the bullfight we went to
not in the city
but in a little village
They don't kill the bull
in Portugal
and they fight on horseback

not on foot as in Spain
I fooled the protocol
The President burst out laughing
when I told him of our hanky panky
The President of Portugal my child
burst out laughing
(*Kisses her on the cheek.*)
The country girl
who came to the city
and made the President happy
my little country lass
my little lass from the country
from that cold dark mountain village
Because she has talent
and energy
That's what's most important
sooner or later
but never too late
you must have talent
at the right moment
and what's even more important my child
you must recognize that talent
before the age of twenty one
and you must get others
to recognize it too
the world must also see that talent
my child
and you must have
one specific talent
because you must
concentrate
on this one talent only
And you must focus
all your energies
on fulfilling
that one just discovered talent
Fulfillment my child
is what it's all about
No pussyfooting my child
the mind must be set only
on fulfilling that talent
that's the only way to make it
Don't ever let them confuse you
the person who has recognized his talent
must constantly remind himself

especially someone in your situation
who first had to realize I must leave
my parents
my mountains
leave for the city
and head for the stage
the only place where such a talent
can grow
Acting my child
is not the kind of art
that develops slowly
it is instant art
A talent the moment it is recognized
has also reached its fulfillment
everything else is nonsense my child
I myself
as everyone knows
come from the very bottom
not from the country
but from the bottom nonetheless
Just like you from the very bottom
and I was way below twenty
when I first recognized my talent
not just any talent
but a political talent my child
I wasn't ten yet
when I realized
that I was a political talent
through and through
While you had the artist already in you
and you also recognized your artistic gifts
just in time
with just the right energy to eliminate
all obstacles
with methods suited to your talent
First one's head must be clear
Your head needs clarity you understand
And ruthlessness which you need to achieve
that clarity inside your head
ruthlessness especially toward yourself
A break with old habits
traditions
with everything
that's in the way of your talent
no mean feat my child

to develop
to become yes to personify
art
Because from the moment
a talent is recognized as such
it must waste no time to develop
And the courage
to offend the world around you
to offend everyone
is an absolute must
Suddenly you have to do
what you've never been able to do
you must be ready to kill
for your talent
for your art
And no sentimentalities my child
and no magic
it doesn't happen by magic
(*Empties his glass and refills it.*)
And such a person can't give a damn
about anything else
you understand
nothing else counts
And the will power
When I suddenly had the idea
to turn political
to become a political person
and I showed up in public with that idea
all by myself exposed to the public with nothing
but that one idea
And you've told yourself
I will be an actress
naturally a great actress a famous actress
a world famous actress
the roads of politics are the same
as the roads of art
paved with brutality
and ruthlessness
and you'll make it to the best the most famous
the most prestigious theatre my child
(*Kisses her on the cheek.*)
Your goal can't be set high enough
always the highest goal
no goal below the highest goal my child
always the highest

If a politician
then President
President of the Republic
Dictator
If an actress
then the greatest
the greatest
the greatest
Such obsession
which might prove a deadly obsession
unthinkable
unbelievable
in the eyes of the public
But who are those people
who is that public
such a person must always say to himself
who are they compared to my talent
my will power
who are they and be it the whole world
to challenge my goal
(*Empties his glass, gets up and opens another bottle.*)
President of the Republic
my child
(*Pours himself and the Actress another glass.*)
You must know your strong points
and use them
against your shortcomings
you must destroy your weak spots
with your own strength
again and again
strength versus weakness
as you fight your way through all the political
all the artistic refuse
The world is refuse
that's all
That I became Minister
at such an early age
officer
Minister
and married that wealthy woman
met and married her
and with her her social circles
This was only a stepping stone
a stepping stone no more
Then life's difficulties multiply

on a steadily rising scale my child
I started out collecting membership fees
for our political party
just as you started out
in summer stock
where genius
discovers itself
And then Metternich
Metternich
Metternich
And Shakespeare for you
Shakespeare again and again
and Goethe
In an unheated room
Your goal always before your eyes
ten years of sleeplessness
and the whole world against you my child
Talent
let alone genius
be it political or artistic
always has the whole world against itself
and it always acts against all reason
it hears what is being said
but it does something different
it hears
and it sees
and it always chooses
the opposite direction
Just as you too have acted against all reason
(*Kisses her on the cheek.*)
Everybody warned you
just as they kept warning me
(*Empties his glass.*)
even though not everyone appreciates your talent
to me you are the greatest
You are the Duse of our time
We'll drink to that
that you're the Duse of our time
(*Fills both their glasses, lifts his glass.*)
All at once
all at once
all at once my child
(*Both empty their glasses, refill both glasses.*)
To my Duse
And I may call myself

a man of some importance
　　　I've received every or nearly every medal of honor
　　　I've received the Papal Order of Sylvester
　　　I've received all Papal Orders
ACTRESS:
　　　You are the greatest
　　　of all statesmen
　　　of all politicians
PRESIDENT:
　　　Statesmen
　　　politicians
ACTRESS:
　　　The greatest
PRESIDENT:
　　　And you are the greatest
　　　actress of our time
　　　If only our country
　　　were bigger than it is
　　　it would match
　　　my potential
　　　(*Lifts his glass and drinks.*)
ACTRESS:
　　　You've achieved everything
　　　there is to achieve in your field
PRESIDENT:
　　　Politics
　　　is the highest form of art my child
　　　higher than the sum total of all the other arts
　　　it is an invisible art
　　　but it keeps changing the world incessantly
　　　The art of acting comes right after
ACTRESS:
　　　And right after that
PRESIDENT:
　　　After that comes painting
　　　Rembrandt
　　　Rubens
　　　Delacroix
ACTRESS:
　　　And after that
PRESIDENT:
　　　Literature my child
　　　literature
　　　and music
　　　music my child

But I am not an expert
in the arts
As far as I'm concerned
the art of politics
is the highest and greatest of all arts
Caesar
Napoleon
Metternich my child
(*Lifts his glass.*)
Metternich
to Metternich
(*Actress lifts her glass.*)
To Metternich
(*They drink.*)
And you must always
and always at the same time
be both practitioner
and theoretician
I would have done much better
in a different epoch
in a time
where I could have become
what I was meant to be
in our time
I cannot realize
what really is inside my head

ACTRESS:
You are a dictator

PRESIDENT:
A dictator
a dictator
Our country is too small for me
Our nation is too small for me
everything is much too narrow and too small for me
Someone with my potential
is always moving in circles there
My head is bound to shrink there

ACTRESS:
Dictator

PRESIDENT:
This country doesn't deserve my husband
my wife once said
to the Ambassador of Mexico
I wish I'd been born in another
completely different country

    and had become the President
    of a completely different country
    (*Drinks.*)
    But now
    suddenly
    Those anarchists my child
    Constantly on the alert
    I live on the edge of death
    everyone lives on the edge of death
ACTRESS:
    The edge of death
PRESIDENT:
    Because I loosened
    the reins
    The Church
    The clergy
    Hoodlums
    A hoodlum nation my child
    How easily it could have been me
    instead of the colonel
    Many attempts my child
    to eliminate me
    But before they eliminate me
    a lot of anarchists will be eliminated first
    Eliminated
    eliminated
    (*Empties his glass, refills it.*)
    Our country is dying
    for the sort of man
    who'll bring back law and order
    order my child
    that's all
    plain order my child
    creating order
    out of this horrendous disorder
    that's spreading everywhere
    and poisons everything
    everything
    On the other hand
    we are quite happy now
    (*Kissing her on the cheek.*)
    that we've found peace and quiet here
    Here we have peace and quiet
    The Atlantic coast
    the coastal climate

(*Suddenly.*)
They still haven't caught those anarchists
What kind of police is this
ACTRESS:
More and more terrorist attacks
PRESIDENT:
You know
it's a disaster my child
What kind of Interior Minister is this
If by tomorrow morning
they haven't cracked down on those anarchists
cracked down my child cracked down
I'll replace both
the Interior Minister and the Chief of Police
ACTRESS:
You'll replace them
PRESIDENT:
Replace them
Replace the whole government
Another government
a new government
(*Lifts his glass, indicates to the Actress she should lift hers, they both lift their glasses.*)
At a hairsbreadth my child
I wouldn't be in Estoril now
The assassination is the reason
for my being here
You've had a shock
my wife said
why don't you go to Estoril
she said
She only said it
so that I would leave
so that she could go to the mountains
with the butcher
Or with the chaplain
The butcher
or the chaplain
I don't care with whom she goes to the mountains
as long as I am here with you my child
(*Drinks.*)
Two thousand policemen
for my personal protection
And you my child

my little diva
with her Foreign Service passport
enjoying the personal protection
of the President
Day after tomorrow we'll go to Sintra
and have some very official fun
Did I shout at that waiter
in Sintra last year
did I let him have it
first in French
which he didn't understand
then in English
which he didn't understand either
and finally in Portuguese
My wife and I
haven't slept with each other
in twenty years
When she's in bed
she thinks of her butcher
the butcher on the one hand
the chaplain on the other
she's got both in her head
but they both don't fit in her head
yet she can't even lose her mind
in the condition she is in
And if she happens to be with me
she still is with the butcher
or the chaplain
This causes her increasing nervousness
This is also why she keeps torturing
our entire domestic staff
Ambition
hate
fear
that's all
Her dog too became
a nervous wreck
because when her head
could no longer bear the butcher and the priest
she came running to her dog
and said that between her two lovers
her spiritual and her physical lover
her dog still meant the most to her
At her age my child

it's a dangerous game with perversion
which is most acute
in a person like her
Now she has lost her dog
I always hated
that useless animal
I hate all useless life
I am not an animal lover
I don't like people or animals
Those four-legged bodies
too spoiled even to bark
just lying around for decoration
waiting to be fed
for nothing
(*Exclaims.*)
The dog dropped dead
from a heart attack
when the colonel became the victim
of a terrorist attack
of that first shot aimed at me
that killed him instantly
the dog became the victim
of a heart attack
Two innocent victims
the colonel and the dog
(*Exclaims.*)
She ran to the coroner's lab
to her dog
The colonel
who laid next to the dog
on the same dissecting table
was of no interest to her
What a repulsive stench
that dog used to leave everywhere
Our bedroom reeked with his stench
the whole palace reeked
of that dog
What a nauseating stench
Small and useless
and no pedigree
From the Humane Society
And chauffered to the Palace
in the Presidential limousine
And then for days weeks months

nothing but that dog
The kitchen a bloody battlefield
because of the dog's menus
An abandoned mutt my child
an abandoned mutt ran the Presidential Palace
for a while
Her husband went through hell with her
but her dog got spoiled to death
The colonel's death didn't faze her
nothing tragic about that
we all must die don't we yes but
that poor little dog
She hated to go to the colonel's funeral
but she gave a great deal of thought
to the dog's proper burial rites
should she bury or burn him
that was her problem
Obsessed by the thought
of ending up alone in any event
she dedicated herself
to the dog
and to money
supported by the chaplain's
idiotic philosophy
He of all people dares to lecture
about innocent lives
about tragedy and greatness of spirit
and she parrots whatever he says
she doesn't understand what he says
but she parrots it
if the chaplain says all men are equal
she parrots it
if the chaplain speaks of spiritual strength
she parrots it
She parrots everything he says
about socialism
religion
philosophy
science
And if he climbs up a mountain and looks down from the top
she'll climb with him and look down too
But he's too dumb for a spy
that frocked idiot
driving women crazy

      The butcher attracts her with his vulgarity
      I saw him once
      leaving through the backdoor
      down the fire escape
      just as I came in
      at two thirty in the morning
      after the ballet
ACTRESS:
      After the ballet
PRESIDENT:
      Swanlake
      Swanlake
      It was Swanlake
      He was in his butcher coat
      he appeared at the Presidential Palace
      in his butcher coat
      mind you
      at the Presidential Palace in a butcher coat
      When she's chewing her food
      ever so slowly
      all that time staring over my head
      at Lucas Cranach on the wall behind me
      she's thinking only of the butcher
      in his butcher jacket
      In company she is absent minded
      because she always has the butcher in her head
ACTRESS:
      Or the chaplain
PRESIDENT:
      Or the chaplain
      She knows I hate the chaplain
      that's why we keep having him for lunch
      I get to the table
      who sits there the chaplain
      always with a book clutched to his breast
      from which he proceeds to read to us
      and it always is an insult
      some religious frivolity
      Then only the very best is being served
      It looks so good
      with that blot of priestly black
      seated at one end of the table
      Sometimes he can be quite amusing
      when he talks about missionaries
      for example
      or the slaughter of nuns in Ethiopia
      Quite a good filler

of conversational gaps
He never leaves without my wife
secretly slipping him a check
When I shake his hand
I hear a check
rustling in his breast pocket
Four or five
toward Christmas even six digit figures
A clever bastard
still peddling the poverty of his Church
Winters in St. Moritz
rubbing elbows with the jet set
in the most obnoxious manner
and always in civilian clothes of course
my wife is there too
she lets him wax her skis
either the chaplain
or the butcher
Whatever there once was between my wife and me
has long since turned to ice
(*Pathetically.*)
It is that icy chill
inside and between all men
Everything just a facade
and the chaplain and the butcher
make a fine pair of
facade climbers
(*Actress laughs out loudly.*
Both laugh and repeat.)
Facade climbers
(*President gets up, opens another bottle of champagne, pours it.*)
Everything is bearable in Estoril
my child
she worships the chaplain
and sleeps with the butcher
The chaplain already pocketed
hundreds of thousands
She spends nothing on herself
but the chaplain gets a fortune
(*Pathetically.*)
The President's wife is a whore
a whore
(*After a pause.*)
A whore reduced to staring
into an empty dog basket
staring you understand
just staring

staring into
an empty dog basket
(*Both empty their glasses.*)
It is a spectacle my child
with a constantly changing cast
of the most impossible people
in most impossible configurations
and possibly
this is the revolution
as the chaplain says
after forty years
revolution is inevitable
inevitable my child
Revolution
slaughter
destruction
(*Drawing out each syllable.*)
destruction
you understand
A deadly spectacle
the scum makes of itself
as night falls
the scum
(*Knocks his glass over, puts it back in its place.*)
of the earth
(*Refills his glass. Suddenly:*)
Crackdowns
liquidations
Your destiny
is similar to mine
We both know the secret to this kind of life
because we created it ourselves
on our own
stupid vicious parents on the one hand
a stupid vicious world on the other
And nothing but unkindness
only unkindness my child
One pair of socks every two years
and for years not enough money
to write a letter to Santa Claus you know
And as you once said
(*Lifts his glass.
She lifts her glass.*)
the aroma of holiday turkeys
only through the windows of the rich
The world is a pigsty
my child
a pigsty

nothing but a pigsty
smut
nothing but smut
So you toughen
and your character toughens
coming up the way we did
Now what does that Artistic Director
have in mind for you
the lead or a small part
Don't worry about the lead my child
You are my leading lady
Never mind playing your small parts
on the stage
(*Kisses her on the cheek.*)
as long as you're my leading lady
(*Suddenly pathetically, lifting his glass.*)
You are the greatest actress
I know
this is why you're my leading lady
you are playing the greatest role
any actress has ever played
on any stage
My leading lady
My little leading lady
My lovely little leading lady
(*Throws his champagne in her face.*)
My leading lady
My lovely little leading lady

Curtain.

Scene 4

A private room in the casino.
President, Portuguese Officers, Ambassador at the table, Colonel near the door to the gambling hall.
Noise of gambling activities from next door.

PRESIDENT: (*Drinking with the others, smoking a cigar.*)
    If you can picture
    the colonel next to me
    and suddenly he's gone
    gone
    gone
    the man is gone
    (*Noises from the gambling hall.*)
    Just because I raised my cane
    toward the Unknown Soldier's Memorial
    To show my wife the bluejay on top
    of the Unknown Soldier's Memorial
    Unusual at this time of year gentlemen
    Then a shot rips through the air
    of uncertainty
    you understand
    Southerly winds
    strong southerly winds
    faltering breaths all around gentlemen
    And that very moment the colonel collapses
    my adjutant
    whom you knew from his many visits
    A gray day gentlemen
    Southerly winds
    strong southerly winds
    A second shot in the air
    And the anarchists are gone
    (*Puffs on his cigar.*)

Gone
Shot from behind the bushes
And that first shot
that hit the colonel
but was meant for me
also killed my wife's dog
the animal had a heart attack
in her arms
She immediately drops the animal
it is dead imagine
holding a dead animal
(*Noises from the gambling hall.*)
I turn around at once
no trace of the assassins
We live dangerously
always on the edge of death gentlemen
My wife starts running
ripping her suit
as she's running through the bushes
Then the guards arrive
Only fifty feet from the Presidential Palace
gentlemen
The colonel was dead on the spot
A shot through the heart
The dog had a heart attack
the colonel was shot through the heart
The assassin must have fired from behind the bushes

OFFICER:
    We don't have any anarchists Mr. President

PRESIDENT:
    As they were dragging the colonel
    his bleeding corpse
    into the Palace
    you must imagine blood everywhere
    I noticed
    that man's chest was ripped apart
    (*To the Ambassador.*)
    They'd ripped apart
    the chest of that man
    who once was your attache
    in Ankara

AMBASSADOR:
    In Ankara Mr. President

PRESIDENT:
    An incorruptible man
    remember
    Related to the Archbishop of Trier

AMBASSADOR:
    And to the Archbishop of Gurk
PRESIDENT:
    And to the Archbishop of Gurk
    That bullet gentlemen
    tore into his body
    passed through the heart
    and came out on the other side
    (*Puffs on his cigar.*)
    I have seen many men die
    but
    They also brought the dog
    to the Presidential Palace
    and laid him next to the colonel
    until the coroners arrived
    My wife went into shock
    The coroner first examined
    the colonel
    then the dog
    (*Noises from the gamnling hall.*)
    My wife locked herself up
    for several hours
    I had a meeting with the Chancellor
    less than half an hour after
    the assassination
    When I left the Chancellor
    all flags were already half mast
    I ordered a state funeral for the colonel
    But to this hour
    the assassins are still at large
OFFICER:
    We don't have assassins in Portugal
PRESIDENT:
    Naturally the assassination
    was a shock to my wife
    It was her idea
    that I should go to Portugal
    a good idea
    wouldn't you say gentlemen
AMBASSADOR:
    An excellent idea Mr. President
PRESIDENT:
    You go to Portugal
    I said to myself
    a few days at the Inglaterra
    you try any place in the world gentlemen
    you won't find a better hotel anywhere

the Inglaterra is the best hotel
in the world
Every other day now
and I'm not exaggerating
we're having a funeral
and once a week
a state funeral
At a hairsbreadth
it would have been me
Don't forget to bring me
a bottle of port
my wife told me
(*To the Ambassador.*)
And our dear Ambassador
has arranged everything
to my greatest satisfaction
(*To the Officers.*)
Our Ambassador is
one of our ablest men
I often think
a man such as he
shouldn't be wasted
at the Atlantic shore
(*Actress enters from the gambling hall.*)
You didn't lose
did you my child
(*To the others.*)
She always wins
She is a great actress
a leading lady gentlemen
(*Actress kisses the President on the forehead.*)
and a great actress
(*Everyone laughs.*)
Only her Artistic Director
a rather unsophisticated
limited man
doesn't know it
he doesn't know her real talent
She's always playing parts
which are completely wrong for her
she is always
miscast
if she gets cast you can bet
she is miscast
It's her agent's fault she says
She should play queens
clever gorgeous queens

or kinky whores
kinky whores
(*He laughs.*
Everybody laughs.)
A tragic role
gentlemen
in a classic tragedy
or a kinky part
in a modern comedy
(*Takes out his wallet and gives her several bills of money for the chips.*)
Here my child
take it my child
maybe you'll have better luck this time
(*To the others.*)
Fortune's child gentlemen
she is Fortune's child
an abandoned child from the Alps
(*Actress kisses the President on the forehead.*
President puts his wallet away.)
An alpine foster child
Great gentlemen
just great
great in every respect
(*To the Actress.*)
How lovely you are
you get lovelier
by the hour
as time goes by
and all the others get uglier
uglier and uglier
the later the hour the uglier
you get lovelier and lovelier
a lovely face
isn't it gentlemen
nature at its loveliest
(*Actress presses the money to her breasts.*)
Self taught
gentlemen
self taught
She never studied acting
but who among the great performers
who among the greatest actresses
had ever studied acting
(*To the Actress.*)
You are self taught
self taught is what you are
(*To the others.*)

She is all rhythm
music
dance
In our acting schools
every talent gets nipped in the bud
The greatest talents are suffocating
in our acting schools
within the shortest period of time
suffocating gentlemen
suffocating
(*Actress leaves for the gambling hall.*
President looking after her.)
A born work of art
definitely a work of art
with an exquisite vocal instrument
and the most perfect technique gentlemen
Last year when she toured England
she enchanted every one of those
cold hard deadly British cities
enchanted is the word yes enchanted
Self taught you must remember
under the humblest of circumstances
Her grandfather worked in a brick kiln
her father was foreman in the same brick kiln
And her mother came from
a ladle carving family
(*Laughs.*)
From a long line of ladle carving
mountain people gentlemen
Today she is a real primadonna
Because she turned down
her Artistic Director's advances
he won't give her a chance
no chance gentlemen
not a chance
The Artistic Director of Europe's largest theatre
of Europe's most prestigious theatre
won't give her a chance
not a chance
She is condemned to idleness
because the Artistic Director won't give her
a chance
only because the Artistic Director
had the wrong idea
about her
as you will agree
undeniably enchanting body

A theatrical body gentlemen
A theatrical body
The Artistic Director's misguided instincts
work to my advantage
since she isn't performing gentlemen
she is with the President of the Republic
traveling around the world
around the world gentlemen
(*Noises from the gambling hall.*)
Now she participates
in my pleasures
Who says we came here
for political discussions
Besides
there are no open ended questions
between our two countries
I only hope that in the meantime
our police haven't been idle
My wife loves the Alps
gentlemen
I am crazy about the Atlantic
she loves classic comedy
I prefer grand opera
Carmen
and let me tell you
my wife hides her money
in handknitted socks
(*Puffs on his cigar.*)
She learned that
from her family
who immigrated
from Switzerland
Now she lives in constant fear
a crippling fear
if you ask me
of anarchists
And she surrounds herself
with doctors and priests
in the belief that they will help her
escape the danger
of going crazy or getting sick
or getting sick a-n-d
going crazy
(*Noises from the gambling hall.*)
as if it did any good
to associate with doctors
and priests

for in such company all roads
lead straight to hell
straight down to a still more radical
and all the more ludicrous end
I've always had the greatest mistrust
towards doctors and priests
life's grand spoilsports
who make or break us gentlemen
And from the very start
I've been against all sciences
not to mention philosophy
if it exists at all
All the more so if we are
and more often than not we indeed are
dealing with a medical minister
that is a doctor playing priest
or a priest playing doctor
(*Puffs on his cigar.*)
because doctors usually claim
that they are the real priests
just as priests maintain
that they are the true doctors
and the world hinges
on this lunacy gentlemen
Yet those two types
are the real destroyers
of all physicality
and all spirituality
(*Noises from the gambling hall.*)
beware above all
of doctors and priests
gentlemen
and mistrust even the greatest mistrust
still implies a lost tie
to their likes
which is another foolish mistake
Women walk right into their trap
every day they'll drag a chaplain
into their rooms
and they'll see a doctor
at least once a week
but they won't let a doctor
tranform their bodies
into some crazy advertisement
of rediscovered health
and they won't let a cleric
drill religion into them

oh no
they let their priests prescribe
their medication
and their doctors describe
heaven and hell to them
and all they get out of either
is their constant fear of the end
Nothing more unbearable than an aging woman
who doesn't know what to do with her aging
who keeps running
from her priests to her doctors
her head stuffed with medicinal herbs
flooded with medical litanies
and religious rubbing alcohol
who keeps running all week
to her doctors and priests
in the hope that she can stop
the process of deterioration
the inevitable course of nature
which she's beginning to realize
and tries to stop by defying
her own nature
(*Points to the door leading to the gambling hall.*)
That's why youth
a young life such as hers
which I've pulled up from the pits
feels so refreshing
refreshing gentlemen
a refreshment
a true refreshment
(*Noises from the gambling hall.*)
When I hear of something
that defies all reason
I think
I must have misunderstood
but it was the truth
A man like me often wishes
he were a complete unknown
and had nothing to do with
what he is doing
with what he is
that it didn't concern him at all
But that he actually is
what everybody says he is
torments this kind of man the most
Yet if he tries to withdraw
inside his own head

he will succeed only
for the shortest period of time
Immediately
he will be running away
from his own head again
(*Puffs on his cigar.*)
Or consider a great artist
an outstanding scientist
always the focus of public attention
But we've put ourselves up on that tightrope
of public suspicion and contempt
Since I am no longer able
no longer that is
than for the shortest time
to disappear inside my head
I must occasionally go away
away gentlemen
away
to Portugal for instance
which I love
I can feel it coming
weeks in advance
At first just the thought
away
away
then with sudden urgency
to the Atlantic coast
to pleasant surroundings
whenever things get most unpleasant
a place where it is possible to move
without danger
without the constant threat
of getting shot
a place to eat and drink in peace
and very well indeed
(*Drinks.*)
How lucky you are gentlemen
so much land still untouched
so many cities still unsoiled
by political mass delusion
while all of Central Europe is losing
its political mind
you keep amusing yourselves the way
Central Europe used to amuse itself
fifty years ago
gentlemen
(*Noises from the gambling hall.*)

amusing gentlemen
amusing
where I come from gentlemen
people forgot
that life has much in common
with grand opera
the world is not a philosophy gentlemen
I hear voices on a stage
I see great entrances
choruses gentlemen
with just a few memorable soloists
and I keep thinking
the backdrop of our world is hung
on an absolutely shock absorbent grid
A man of such uncompromising singlemindedness
has no purpose other than
himself
the politician just like the artist
went his own way
all by and only for himself
and what he went through
he forgot
The man who panics on his way
cannot be helped
He has swept along so many
too many to count
swept along gentlemen
swept along
swept along
Because you never had a war here
gentlemen
no eruptions gentlemen
absolutely no eruptions
And because you have everything
so nicely under control
You make no room for anarchists gentlemen
(*Actress returns from the gambling hall indicating that she has lost all the money.*
President immediately pulls out his wallet, takes out a wad of bills, which he holds up in the air, exclaiming:)
Everything I own
gentlemen
(*Actress goes to him, takes the money, kisses him on the forehead, and exits to the gambling hall.*)
You make no room for anarchists
gentlemen

Your many prisons are the backbone
of law and order
(*Noises from the gambling hall.*)
If people live too well
they develop megalomania
and the lunatics
set the nation on fire
People develop megalomania
and lose their minds
They can no longer be restrained
and everything heads toward chaos
History proves everything
gentlemen
the greatest idiot can see
that history proves everything
The people must be distracted
from history gentlemen
to keep all proofs away from them
(*Noises from the gambling hall.*)
Only the dilettante
will miss that point
gentlemen
the dilettante
and then she
my wife
is constantly afraid
that her own son
will shoot me
or that he will shoot
his own mother
Yes our son
became an anarchist
and one of the most dangerous
I have to be afraid
of my own son
gunning me down
or bludgeoning me
gentlemen
some day some time gentlemen
At night my wife keeps talking
about our son
being our killer
his whole life comes down
to this one threat
Parents produce a son
they raise him

and they realize
that they have raised their murderer
A man with such precise knowledge
of his parents
who by nature gentlemen
can only hate his procreator
Our son is predestined
predestined I say
to kill us
(*Puffs on his cigar.*)
What is it I ask myself
that drives this kind of man
to suddenly want to destroy himself
to aim for destruction
rather than growth
by leaving
and he doesn't care
where he's going
then all of a sudden
he kills himself
out of fear
or he kills his parents
out of fear
or he goes underground
to get himself destroyed
because the man who can't be helped
will be destroyed in any case
If we had strength
our son doesn't
If we created order
our son didn't
if we in time at least I think
found happiness
our son didn't
if we could gradually
pull ourselves up
by our own agonizing heads
our son didn't
And if we finally woke up
our son didn't
have anything to do with it
At night I keep thinking
how someone like him
can run off and ruin himself
while we don't know where he is
he is here

suddenly
and destroys us
and he destroys himself
at night I keep thinking
he will do it
he will do it
he will do it gentlemen
(*Gets up and says:*)
Let's win it all back
To the gambling hall gentlemen
(*Exclaims.*)
let's win it all back
win back what I lost
(*Throws his full glass against the wall and leaves for the gambling hall, everybody looking after him.*)

Curtain.

Scene 5

Great Hall.
Funeral music by Beethoven.
The President is laid out in state.
His face is visible through a large glass window on the coffin.
Two Funeral Attendants under an Officer's supervision put two candelabras next to the bier.

ATTENDANT 1: (*Adjusting the black cloth one last time.*)
   There
   there
ATTENDANT 2:
   There
   there
   (*Both Attendants exit.*)
OFFICER: (*Loudly, pathetically.*)
   The bier is now ready for viewing
   (*The door opens.*
   First Lady, veiled, enters, supported by the Chaplain. She stops in front of the bier, looks in and exits left.
   After the First Lady, Members of the Government.
   After the Members of the Government, the Diplomats.
   After the Diplomats, the People.*)

Curtain.

EVE OF RETIREMENT

Eve of Retirement was first performed on September 24, 1981, by the Guthrie Theater, Minneapolis. It was directed by Liviu Ciulei. The cast included:

RUDOLF HOELLER / *Donald Madden*
CLARA / *Catherine Burns*
VERA / *Betty Miller*

Set: Jack Barkla
Costumes: Jared Aswegan
Lighting: Paul Scharfenberger

Characters

RUDOLPH HOELLER, Chief Justice and former SS Officer
CLARA, his sister
VERA, his sister

Place

The house of Chief Justice Hoeller

ACT I

What is character but the determination of incident.
                                        Henry James

Large room on the first floor.
Two high windows in the back, a door on either side.
Various chairs, easy chairs, a dresser, an ironing board at the window, a piano.
Late afternoon on October 7, Himmler's birthday.

VERA: (*Closing the door on the left.*)
  She's gone
CLARA: (*In a wheelchair, mending her brother's socks.*)
  Are you sure
VERA:
  She's going to her grandmother
  and will stay until tomorrow
  Poor child
  with her coughing fits
  But if we put her in an institution
  she'll waste away
  this place is good for her
  this place is like home to her
  (*Moves her right index finger across one of the window sills.*)
  dust everywhere
  dirt
  (*Looks at the barometer.*)
  It's way down
  it's falling
  She could use a little sun
  but since she's going to her grandmother
  it doesn't make any difference anyway
  It's not easy for me either
  with an illiterate
  It's really an art
  dealing with a deaf mute
  at her age they are so stubborn on top of it

especially when they come from the country
and don't know anything
(*Pulls at the curtain.*)
here she's certainly treated
with kid gloves
(*Looks through the window.*)
It's always gloomy on this day
But that adds a certain solemnity
I've already chilled three bottles of champagne
Fuerst Von Metternich the brand Rudolph likes so much
(*Starts to iron Rudolph's judge's robe, which has been hanging on the wall.*)
He has reached the highest position
a judge can reach
he is afraid of retirement
Our Olga is a blessing
for him too
he enjoys her
she's nice to look at
after all
If you only knew
where I dredged her up
that such poor squalid conditions
still exist even today
But these people have only themselves to blame
for their misery
Poverty is no longer necessary
Poverty is caused
by the poor themselves
Don't ever help the poor
father used to say
you pull them out of their filth
but it won't do any good
I had two pretty dresses made for her
she wanted one in baby blue
but that was out of the question
one black and one dark brown
very pretty very pretty
I tied her braids exactly the way
I used to wear them
remember
how mother tied our braids
very slowly
and always with a bit of advice
Sometimes I think of myself
when I look at that child
when she's by herself and thinks no one is watching

she sits on the floor and plays with her hands
either with her hands or with her braids in turns
CLARA:
We are only exploiting her
It's disastrous for her
to be here
We only ruin this child
She'll collapse one day
You knew what you were doing
when you chose a deaf mute
for a maid
VERA:
You always think the worst of me
That's your habit
That's your weapon against me
(*Looks out the window.*)
Of course someone who can hear and talk
would certainly be better in a way
On the other hand it's lucky
that she can't hear that she can't talk
everything hinges on just that
that she cannot hear or talk
imagine if she could talk
if she could hear
CLARA:
Out of pity
you keep saying
but that too is a perversion
VERA:
Maybe
maybe you're right
Soon it will be my last time
to iron his robe
Then we'll take a trip
to the sea
The three of us
CLARA:
You exploited every one of your maids
until they collapsed
then you discarded them
Deaf and mute
the ideal tool
for your mental and emotional paralysis
VERA:
When I look at you
What gives you the right

to talk to me like that
for years I've put up with everything
you said
CLARA:
She's here primarily for you
you take up all her time
she knows full well
that if she suddenly
could hear and speak
you would kill her instantly
VERA:
Sometimes I feel
like wheeling you up a cliff
up there where it's the steepest
and pushing you off
into the water
with all your misery
CLARA:
That's all you can think of
But you keep controlling yourself
Control means everything to you
just like father
your life depends on it
in fact you don't really live at all
you just drag yourself from lie to lie
VERA:
When she's with her grandmother
she is in good care
I don't have to worry about her
I know everything is fine
when she's with her grandmother
CLARA:
Wouldn't you love to run after her
and check
if she really went
to her grandmother
VERA:
Where else could she go
poor thing
CLARA:
What if some day
she won't be going to her grandmother
what if she suddenly were able to talk
VERA:
You and your vicious imagination

CLARA:
    You always had luck
    with your maids
    they all came from the country
    poverty cases as they say
VERA:
    Where would you be without her
    as long as I want her here
    and as long as she can manage
    she'll be at our disposal
    at your disposal
    to be more exact
    Her illness isn't all that bad
    an occasional fit
    She has become much calmer
    As long as we keep her busy
    People who work don't get sick
    She just has to have something to do
    all the time
    keep her busy
    and she'll get better
    not worse
CLARA:
    She is terrified
VERA: (*Laughs.*)
    Terrified
    is that so
    she was less than human
    when she first got here
    she was nothing nothing
    a zero
    Your pity for her is also
    a weapon against me
    Father saw right through
    that so-called solidarity with servants
    and called it by its proper name
    vulgarity
    I only want what's best for you
    as long as she is here
    this household functions
    otherwise everything would fall apart
    and you would be institutionalized at once
    that you are here at all is only possible
    because of her
    don't you forget it

She's literally blossomed
since she's come here
She wouldn't be alive any more
without my kindness
I am her teacher
and I even pay her very well
I pay her more than she deserves
but that's not the point
Here she has everything she needs
At home she has nothing
All that socialist talk everywhere
yet nothing has changed
basically
A primitive vulgar mother
running around in rags
An alcoholic father
eight brothers and sisters choking on their own dirt
because they're too lazy to wash themselves
So much bodily filth
is bound to suffocate the soul
as father used to say
I pulled that child out of the muck
and she has changed to her advantage
Born into that proletarian filth
she would have choked on it
very soon very soon
believe me
if I hadn't come along
The parents were happy
that I took her on
When I left
her mother kissed me on the cheek
it was repulsive
The child was happy
as soon as she set foot
in this house
CLARA:
  Into this horrible house
VERA:
  She doesn't see it as horrible
  she is grateful
  what she came from
  wasn't fit for humans
  You must put yourself in the place of such simple people
  This is paradise for that kind of person

CLARA:
  This ghastly atmosphere

VERA:
  Your knowledge of human nature
  is not the best
  It comes straight out of books
  and newspapers
  You really have no personal experience
  This child is well off with us
  and it's just as well
  that she is deaf and dumb and can't be cured
  it saves her
  and of course us
  a lot of trouble
  She has learned a lot around here

CLARA:
  You mean she saw a lot around here

VERA:
  You certainly are out of touch with reality
  destructive
  ungrateful
  that's what you are
  Deaf and dumb
  what a blessing
  I don't care
  what she sees
  as long as she doesn't talk about it
  and that she can't do
  Two dresses for her
  and of very expensive material
  while I haven't bought myself a new dress
  in eight years
  The sister of Chief Justice Hoeller
  has been wearing the same dress for years
  I know what people are saying
  it's obvious that they envy me
  they envy Rudolf for everything
  and they wish you the worst
  those hypocrites talk about you
  as if you were a saint
  it's disgusting
  By the way I gave her
  the dressing gown with the red trim
  for her grandmother

CLARA:
    Generous
    Philanthropic
VERA:
    Say what you like
    It's all right
    I love you and protect you
    but it's hard with a person
    who despises me unnecessarily
    who thinks she knows better
    Our lot has not been the worst
    What if Rudolf hadn't returned from the war
    What if they had brought him to trial
    Isn't it nice that everything turned out all right
    We are respected people aren't we
    and we are well off
    Whatever we want
    we can have
    With so much misery in the world
    we can't complain
    we have it good
    we don't have to be afraid
    only you are never content
    always plagued by your obsessions
    I couldn't take care of you myself
    dressing and undressing you three times a day
    it's out of the question
    Rudolf often wonders
    if you wouldn't be better off
    in a sanitarium
    Don't worry
    we wouldn't dare
    The three of us are a conspiracy
    aren't we
    You have the best life here
    you don't lack anything
    you have everything you need
    nice surroundings
    helpful people
    who love you
    you always get
    your wishes
    this we owe one another
    to always grant each other every wish
    all in all it's an ideal mechanism
    you and I and Rudolf

Things could be much worse
(Picks up the robe and holds it against the light.)
We are full of affection for one another
(Looks out.)
It will all stay the same
once he retires
Once we start traveling
Rudolf wants to go to Egypt
We will even find a way
for you to come along
all four of us will go
Olga will be all yours
Who has it easy nowadays
(Directly to Clara.)
No no that child is in good hands here
but you mustn't confuse her
you terrify her
leave her alone
be happy she's here
she does her work
that's all
You're always racking your brains
over trifles
You haven't changed
We don't need a witness on October seventh
(Takes the robe, hangs it on the wall, looks it over.)
Days before the seventh
Rudolf starts to change
everything in him is geared toward the seventh
(Takes the robe off the wall, puts it back on the ironing board and continues ironing.)
He talked to Himmler only once
a man who wasn't to be contradicted
and Rudolf swore that as long as he lives
he would celebrate Himmler's birthday
That he never married
has something to do with this
None of us can get away
(Suddenly directly to Clara.)
And just before October seventh
you keep having those strange dreams
(Questioning her.)
You always wake up
just before he crushes you to death

CLARA:
    At first I thought

it was an animal
but then it was a man after all
VERA:
Well just consider your condition my dear
CLARA:
A huge animal you know
a wild animal
completely covered with hair
and it gets bigger and bigger
and I can't get away
I am afraid he will crush me to death
But the moment he crushes me
I wake up
VERA:
You always dream of a man
crushing you to death
that's your condition my dear
it's at its worst on October seventh
it's quite obvious that you are afraid
the man will crush you to death
CLARA:
I faint and then I wake up
VERA:
You still haven't asked him
for his name
it's of utmost importance
that you ask him for his name
CLARA:
No
VERA:
You must ask him
you must ask him immediately
CLARA:
Yes
VERA:
You must ask him
you must confront him
your monster
before it crushes you to death
before it turns into a man
CLARA:
Yes
VERA:
That's the problem
you never ask him for his name
You have to know his name

We simply fell into this that's all
You have to play your part
in your wheelchair you understand
It's always worst before October seventh
but it's also quite wonderful
don't you think so
(*Laughs.*)
You can't fool nature
We keep making the same crucial mistakes
we set up a system for ourselves
and we keep making the same mistakes
(*Suddenly.*)
Shall I wheel you outside
before Rudolf gets home
Afterwards it will be too late you know
For him October seventh
is the most important day of the year
(*Looks out.*)
It's foggy
you can't see a thing
I can't even see the tree
As long as we keep warm inside
and we have enough food
and we have our Olga
we should be content
Another year gone by already
eight years without a new dress
at least on October seventh
to make Rudolf happy
but I don't have the energy
(*Looks out.*)
A dangerous afternoon
Always be on your guard
father used to say
He was right
He would be proud of Rudolf
(*Hangs the finished robe on the wall, examines it, then:*)
And now I'll make us some coffee
You'll have a cup with me won't you
CLARA:
　Yes of course
VERA: (*As she exits.*)
　Our father taught us mistrust
　how fortunate
　that we listened to him
CLARA: (*To herself.*)
　Never suppress mistrust

>   always obey mistrust
>   always approach people with mistrust
>   always listen to nature
> VERA: (*Offstage.*)
>   How right he was
>   we should have listened to him more
>   maybe then he'd still be alive
>   how old would father be today
> CLARA: (*Calling out.*)
>   He wouldn't have liked
>   what happened afterwards
> VERA: (*Calling back.*)
>   What do you mean
> CLARA:
>   You and Rudolf
> VERA:
>   You don't understand
>   It just happened
>   It simplifies so much
>   You have no right
>   to pass judgment
>   it's all to your advantage
>   if things were different
>   if Rudolf were married
>   this way he is with us
>   everything is kept between us
> CLARA:
>   He always praised you
>   he hated me
>   He loved you
>   he hated me
> VERA:
>   How fortunate that you can't walk
>   you'd be in jail by now
>   with your crazy ideas
>   you'd be sitting in some prison
>   That wheelchair saves you
>   from imprisonment
>   Father always knew
>   how dangerous you were
>   Family killer that's what he called you
>   There's some truth to it
>   Our little socialist can consider herself lucky
>   that she can't move
>   they would have caught you long ago
>   locked you up and sentenced you

you would have disappeared
CLARA:
It's in my nature
to be bad
father used to say
He always loved you
VERA:
You'd be dangerous out there
I know you
You'd be throwing bombs
and killing people
everyone you hate
you hate them all
Because you're insane
a fanatic
(*Enters with a tray of coffee and sits down next to Clara.*)
Your tragedy saved you my dear
you owe everything to that air raid to the bombing
Rudolf says so too
you'de be a terrorist by now
CLARA:
What do you know about that
VERA:
From the same parents
yet such completely different children
Be happy you are here
in protective custody so to speak
you are very fortunate
even though everything in you keeps rebelling
that's only natural
this way you are limited
to an occasional nasty letter to the editor
Out there the world is quite different my dear
(*Pours herself and Clara some coffee.*)
Father liked it
when we went to the park
all dressed in white
he'd let us play
and watch us
sometimes he'd call us My Beauties
Mother always wanted to see Paris
it was her obsession
he hated this idea
he always promised
that he'd take her to Paris
but he had no intention of going

Do you think he loved her
Your father does nothing but abuse me she used to say
He is inhuman
I am ashamed for him she used to say
(*Looks at the left door.*)
How dirty these doors are
First thing tomorrow
when Olga comes back
the doors must be cleaned
and the windows
there's so much dust on the window sills
You don't see any of this
but its drives me crazy
You should see the kitchen
and today of all days
Actually everything here disgusts me too
but the mere thought
that something might be changed
In fact this place should be repainted
(*Looks around.*)
See the cracks in the ceiling
they're getting worse
it's an old house
the curtains are gray
everything grimy and gray
We haven't had a visitor in years
because that's how Rudolf wants it
It wouldn't do any harm
to have an occasional visitor
Then again
who would be suitable
Rudolf's cut himself off completely
because of his position
and because in truth he's always been a lonely man
he's always hated company
even though he can be so charming at parties
people are quite surprised
when they see him completely open and relaxed
entertaining a large crowd
who'd be dying of boredom otherwise
he got that from father
who at home was withdrawn
and an absolute tyrant
but a real charmer at parties
it was a big problem for mother
Well from time to time we do get to see the acting Prime Minister

and Professor Wackernagel
I don't care for that boring man
who only talks about his research
which no one understands and which is worthless I'm sure
there's nothing more boring than that kind of scientist
And he started an argument with Doctor Fromm
which is a pity
the doctor always lightened the mood
As soon as the doctor arrived
everyone's spirits began to brighten up
But it's been two years
since the doctor was last here
He's bought himself a beautiful home
Doctors are rolling in money
They are the only ones who can afford to live in luxury today
The true saints as father used to call them
Maybe I should talk to Rudolf
about making up with the doctor again
don't you think it's a shame
that the doctor has stopped coming
Rudolf was jealous that's true
but now he has no more reason
and you
you liked him too
CLARA:
   Maybe
VERA:
   Such people can make a house a home
   they even make the world more livable
CLARA:
   But even people like him finally conform
   they stagnate they grow stale
VERA:
   You should have seen the doctor the other day
   I ran into him downtown
   as he was coming out of the jewelry shop
   he looked more elegant than ever
CLARA:
   I know what you like
VERA:
   You drag everything through the mud
CLARA:
   Through the mud where it belongs
VERA:
   You and your sick views
   You should be pitied my dear

If you could just once see things from a normal perspective
Your revolutionary ruined you
Sometimes I think what a blessing
that he disappeared from your life
It's always so crucial whom one meets
You took up with the devil
Sometimes I think it's just as well
he's dead
He destroyed you that's a fact
He infected your mind
fed you disgusting literature
and completely destroyed you for good
He took the easy way out
a bullet through his head
and not a second thought for you
But just think if you were

CLARA:
Not paralyzed you're about to say

VERA:
Of course
how awful it would be with you
Yet this is the way things are
In the meantime you too got old
it's far better you let me wheel you to his grave
than being dead yourself
The bad ones drag the others down
father used to say
It's a good thing that I have everything
already prepared
Justice Roesch
won't be coming this year
he has a cold
And it's better for Rudolf to be alone
I don't like that man
Colleagues are always dangerous
Perhaps it's just an excuse
A year ago on his way here
he was stopped
harrassed
by some young hoodlums who recognized him from court
and nearly dragged him into a bar with them
luckily he was able to get away
Imagine they had torn off his coat
and he just stood there in his SS uniform
Maybe he feels it's too dangerous this year
he called and said he had a cold
he felt miserable and couldn't come
he would celebrate Himmler's birthday at home by himself

A despicable man really isn't he
But a loyal friend to Rudolf
His lips are sealed you understand
I know you hate me
when I talk like this
But I get so excited
when October seventh comes around
It's Rudolf's obsession
to celebrate this day
After all it was the high point of his life
The time will come Rudolf says
when he'll no longer be forced
to celebrate Himmler's birthday
hiding away in our house
but out in the open my dear
openly quite openly
in front of everyone
Of course it's madness
the way he clings to it
but why should I spoil his fun
We have to support him
Who knows what's ahead of us
We are a conspiracy
It means so much to him
I'm forever grateful to you
that you leave us in peace
I know what this means to you
Then again what else could you do
And in return first thing tomorrow morning
I'll put all your leftist books back on the table again
and buy you all the newspapers you want

CLARA:
You make me sick
but I listen to you
I promised
and you are right
what else can I do
I am at your mercy
It's no secret
that on Himmler's birthday
you two also go to bed together
after the second bottle of champagne
I'm not even embarrassed anymore
My poor sister what else can she do
but submit to her brother's madness
You are still worse off than I
and only because you are such a liar
can you bear to stand it at all

more perverted than your brother
more abominable
much more vicious
(*Vera gets up and exits with the coffee tray.*)
Everything you do is admirable
I admire you
I always admired you
(*Calls after her.*)
my big sister
whom I always admired
(*To herself.*)
We are condemned to viciousness
(*Picks up the pair of socks again, starts mending, calls out.*)
None of us deserves any better
But your perversity beats Rudolf's
by far
(*Vera enters and opens the dresser.*)
I admire you
I really admire you
but I also despise you

VERA:
It's to be expected
You haven't changed
(*Takes a framed picture of Himmler out of the dresser, walks to the window with it and polishes it.*)

CLARA:
You're not to blame
Nobody's to blame

VERA:
What are you talking about
just stop it will you
I know what you really think
(*Breathes on the picture.*)
People are the way they are
and they have to get along with each other
You've learned that too
(*Looks out.*)
Everything grimy and gray
that's the way it was
even when we were children
nothing's changed
Father wouldn't tolerate the slightest change
We are a true lawyer's family
with everything that goes with it you understand
that's not easy
The lawyer's children people used to say
when we walked through town by ourselves
(*Breathes on the picture.*)

This picture was taken
when Himmler visited the camp
Rudolf had lunch with him alone
the day after his thirty-ninth birthday
There was nothing more difficult
than being camp commander
A commander that was the worst
Rudolf was quite impressed
with what Himmler had to say
(*Puts the picture on the window sill, looks at it.*)
And it was Himmler after all
who gave him the forged passport
with which Rudolf disappeared
Rudolf owes it to him
that he is still here
and we owe it to Rudolf
that we are still here
If they had caught him
they would have killed him on the spot
this way he got off
And then ten years later
no one asked any more questions
That's the way it is
(*Takes the picture, exits, and enters again without the picture, walks to the judge's robe, looks it over.*)
Rudolf is a decent man
you know that
If he weren't
we wouldn't live the way we do
People applaud him every time
he talks about love of country
as he did the other day at the Legal Society
Every time he says love and country
he gets applause
They didn't want to see him go
but his retirement can't be put off
(*Looks around.*)
Father wouldn't tolerate the slightest change
and mother acquiesced
women always acquiesce
that won't change
they won't admit it
but they acquiesce
and they don't mind
at first mother resisted that's true
then she gave up
all of a sudden
from one moment to the next

she gave up quickly don't you think
how old and gray she was already at thirty
and ugly quite frankly
then everything happened very quickly
Paris she said again and again
until she stopped saying it
First father ignored her
then she stopped saying it
(*Pulls on the curtain.*)
when she was dead he said
I should have taken her to Paris
How would that have changed anything
I think Paris is dreadful
Everyone wants to see Paris
I always found Paris the ugliest city
a desolate wasteland
they all talk of a Paris
that doesn't exist
better dead than living in Paris
Close to home that's where it's nicest
But they all talk of Paris
because it's been the fashion for two hundred years

CLARA:
She wasn't ugly

VERA:
Mother

CLARA:
Yes

VERA:
She certainly was
On her thirtieth birthday
a horrible sight my dear
You are lucky
because you don't remember
ugly and bitter that's what she was
old and alone
although she lived in our midst
and father was mean and brutal to her
I'm embarrassed to speak of him like that
but it's the truth
(*Holds up the robe.*)
Another six months
and he won't be putting on his robe anymore
His Honor the Chief Justice
it will be hard for him
the older they get our dear men
the vainer they get
of course he says he can't wait for the last time

    he'll be putting on his robe
    but it will be hard on him
    His Honor the Chief Justice
    a long hard climb
    that Paragon of Justice
    as they say
    (*Exits with the robe.*)
CLARA:
    I cleared my own path to the top
    father used to say
    and I didn't soil my hands in the process
    unlike the others
    When we went out
    we had to walk in front of him
    which always frightened us
    (*Calls out.*)
    It's a good thing that mother
    didn't put up with it any longer
    Rudolf was ashamed of her suicide
    What sort of lawyer's family is this
    where the mother kills herself
    Will you bring me the papers
    (*To herself.*)
    We inherit the insecurity
    that drags out our lives
    Hated by father
    because unwanted
    as well as by mother
    (*Vera comes back with a SS officer's uniform and with newspapers, which she gives to her sister.*)
VERA:
    Every day you bury your head
    in this printed filth
    (*Takes the uniform to the ironing board, puts the trousers on the ironing board, hangs the jacket on the window and starts ironing.*)
    All of us killed mother
    she had no resilience
    as father used to say
    she was made of the fragile matter
    which isn't meant for this brutal world
    it didn't take much
    to break her
    (*Directly to Clara.*)
    He didn't want you
    and he didn't love you
    he was a lawyer through and through
    and he would be proud to see Rudolf now
    If he knew

that his children ended up alone
he enjoyed
ceremony
he liked being a soldier an officer
Mother foresaw everything
that's why she broke
And under what circumstances did we end up alone
getting there old and alone
the three of us
that's no coincidence
no doubt about that
(*Clara reads the newspapers.*)
You can't wait
for these obscenities
You devour this printed garbage
and you rejuvenate
It's your only passion
you don't have any others
You live on newspapers
nothing else
you think through newspapers
all your values come straight out of newspapers
Nothing is more abominable
than the newspaper business Rudolf says
selling the crap that goes on nowadays
to people who grab it eagerly
The filthiest papers are published
by the Jews
I know you don't like hearing this
but it's a fact
Your father was a Jew hater
like ninety-eight percent of the population
only very few admit
that they are anti-Semitic
but the Germans hate the Jews
even as they claim just the opposite
that's the German nature
you can't get around it
because you can't get around nature
in a thousand years the Jews will still be hated in Germany
in a million years
if there'll be any Germans or Jews left at all
that's what Rudolf says
(*After a pause.*)
At first it's always an animal
then a large violent man
who crushes you to death
your dreams are a precise reflection

of your condition
you couldn't have any other dreams
My condition isn't much better
(*Looks out.*)
The days are already getting so short
(*Turning toward Clara again.*)
Or do you think that my condition is better
that I'm the lucky winner
you know very well this isn't true
and my going to bed with Rudolf
is the most logical solution
I find it perfectly natural
We are a conspiracy
We close the curtains when it's time
Nobody knows what we're doing
We don't keep any secrets from each other do we
(*Suddenly resolutely.*)
I'll wheel you outside if you want me to
(*Looks out.*)
But that would be silly
it's cold and almost dark
We've been acting our parts for so many years
we can't get out anymore
if they were alive
we might kill them who knows
I've killed mother many times in my dreams
knifing strangling bludgeoning her
You hide your head behind those papers
but I know what you look like
I know your face
you keep on living in your paper world
you won't be bothered
not by the worst monstrosity
not even if I tell you
that I'd kill my mother
if she were still around
This is how you punish me
this is how we punish each other
How I always hated those papers
all those special magazines I got for you
because I can see
how they gradually ruin you
you're disintegrating from all this reading
It clearly shows what this filth does to you
But the point is
that we keep acting our parts
to perfection
sometimes we don't understand it ourselves

then we get scared
but we know full well what we have to do
You and your wheelchair
that's at least as cruel
as I and Rudolf
We can't help ourselves
we keep lying to ourselves
but how nice it is in the end
doing what we do
by acting it
and acting what we act
by doing it
It is no longer possible
to go against our own rules
(*Leaves the ironing board, goes toward Clara and strikes the newspaper away from her face.*)
Your face is already ruined
from your papers
You are even uglier
than our mother
It has all been decided my dear
(*Clara tries to smooth out the paper and read it again.*)
The real art lies in keeping
the ones we hate alive
but just enough to torment them
again and again
without really killing them
(*Irons the trousers.*)
I don't even know
what made me
do it
he didn't resist
your brother
it is quite natural my dear
(*Clara hides her face behind her papers again.*)
You swore
you would never again mention
the names Rosa Luxemburg and Clara Zetkin
you kept your promise
You are one of us all right
and how
We have rehearsed our play
the parts were cast thirty years ago
each of us got his role
a despicable and dangerous one
each got his costume
and woe to the one who slips into the other's costume
The point at which the curtain will come down

must be a joint decision made by the three of us
No one has the right to lower the curtain at will
that's against the law
Sometimes I actually see myself
on a stage
and I am not ashamed in front of the audience
unlike you who is always ashamed
who nearly goes crazy with shame
We only go on
living
because we keep giving each other the cues
you and I and Rudolf
as long as it suits us
we shall see
It's so artificial so cold sometimes
for days
then it eases up again
(*Listens.*)
For a minute I thought I heard Rudolf
He will sit here and suddenly not say a word
and that means
he wants me
to bring him the photo album
I have to turn the pages
and I have to look at it with him
picture after picture
the same every year
he arranged them in perfect order
that orderly man
for every picture he has a story
a horror story
as if his memory
consisted of nothing but piled-up corpses
This album frightens me more
than anything else
Last year he made me
shave your head
and dress you up
as an inmate of a concentration camp
We must do what he wants
He is a sick man of course
or don't you think so
You bury your head in your papers
because you can't run away
(*Looks at the watch.*)
Would you like something to eat
I think we should wait
otherwise we'll spoil our appetite for the birthday dinner

I never knew
that Himmler only lived to be forty
a young idol don't you think
I would have liked to have seen Hamlet
I can't see how you can live without Shakespeare
Hamlet
Our brother the Chief Justice
treats us to the center box
and you say no
a new Hamlet
a famous actor
the one who played the Prince of Homburg
I would have enjoyed it
What would people say
if I were to sit alone in the box
without you
Where did you leave your poor sister
that's what they'd say
I've been through it before
that poor child
who was struck by a ceiling beam
by an American bomb
paraplegic how awful
They are always saying the same thing
I know what everyone's saying
If I go by myself everybody keeps asking for you
Your poor sister where is she
helpless
hopeless
pitiful thing
Everything really depends on you
if you won't see Hamlet
I can't see it either
if you won't go to the concert
I can't go either
if you don't care for art
I won't have it either
and you know how much I need cultural stimulation
At least once a month
if not weekly
a cultural stimulant
My love for the theatre comes from father
my love for music from mother
you deprive me of plays as well as concerts
We used to go to every chamber recital
that was when we still played the cello of course
CLARA: (*Laughs.*)
The cello

When we still played the cello
  how out of key we used to play
  what ghastly amateurs we were
VERA:
  You think so
  I don't
  (*Holds the trousers up against the light.*)
  It was so nice
  when we made music
  (*Looks at the piano.*)
  It must be years
  since I last touched the piano
  Making music
  in this horrible house
  saturating these cold walls with music
  bringing them to life with music
CLARA: (*Cynically.*)
  Saturating with music
  you can't be serious
  to think you managed
  to bring life to this ghastly house
  this morgue
VERA:
  I thought I did
  Even when we were children
  and mother used to play
  on those wonderful long winter evenings
  What a shame that Rudolf
  gave up the violin
  I miss it a lot
  he had such a soft touch
  The war spoiled it for him
  It was so different here
  when we made music together
  (*Goes to the piano, opens it, wants to play something.*)
  No no
  there is no more time to make music
  (*Turns toward Clara.*)
  The arts are a means
  of saving oneself
  but you reject everything beautiful of course
  (*Closes the piano, gets up and goes back to the ironing board.*)
  You reject all means of salvation
  anything that might bring pleasure
  You're shrouded in gloom
CLARA:
  What a liar you are
  how can you be such a liar

you're full of lies and deceit
It was always awful
when our parents were alive
and it was unbearable
when we made music
and nothing has changed
since their deaths
except that the two of you grew more vicious and brutal
you don't even know
what music or art is all about
in your hands music always became
something atrocious
And there was nothing more atrocious
than father reading poetry
how many times did you butcher music
fiction poetry
you always violated art
You always say
when our parents were alive
but nothing has changed
the way you lie
the way you always lied
you always lied to yourself
and to Rudolf and everyone else
The cello how dare you
In your hands it became an abomination
and Rudolf with his violin
I can't think of a greater perversion
It was nothing but a mad idea of our father
and a mad idea of our unfortunate mother
they wanted us to make music
because children from good families always made music
and read fiction and poetry
Deep down father hated music
and he had no idea of Literature
he abhorred poetry
One day he even proved himself stupid enough
to buy a Bosendorfer
he would have done better buying me a pistol instead
to shoot him
to shoot all of you

VERA:
You're insane
just like your father
you're getting more like him every day
I get chills
when I hear you
talk like him

now I know exactly why he hated you
   and vice versa
CLARA:
   Music in this cold house
   in this abominable pit
VERA:
   When he read to us
   we weren't allowed to move
   he always read to us from books
   we didn't understand
   he tortured us with Schopenhauer
CLARA:
   And Nietzsche
VERA: (*Holds up the trousers against the light and continues ironing.*)
   When they are doing Strindberg
   will you go
CLARA:
   No
VERA:
   For months no theatre
   no concert
   I feel like I'm in prison
   (*Suddenly inquisitive.*)
   What are you punishing me for
   What did I do
   If only we could go to court again
   to amuse ourselves
   Not if it's Rudolf case of course
   how about a jury trial
   one of Roesch's
   I don't think Rudolf would mind
   if I tell him
   we need to get out
   you're so pale my dear you look sick
   We're always only dealing with each other
   I with you
   you with me
   and with Rudolf
   You shouldn't hate me dear
   I don't deserve it
   The most interesting trials are coming up now
   In the old days you were always ready to go
   No murder trial without you
   you couldn't wait to go
   Let's go
   we never do anything else
   it's free
   and it's the most exciting entertainment

they made ramps for the handicapped
now I can wheel you right into the courtroom
Let's go there let's
What's the theatre
compared to a trial
(*Goes over to the desk and looks at the calendar.*)
The thirteenth
against Amon
the twenty-second against Harreiter
Amon's the one who killed the industrialist's widow
remember
CLARA:
Of course I remember
VERA:
Harreiter is also Roesch's case
not Rudolf's
we'll go yes we'll go there
we'll have lunch with Rudolf in the court house cafeteria
if he's around
(*Puts the calendar away, goes back to the ironing board to continue with her ironing, looks out the window.*)
The park twice a week
isn't enough
Every day the doctor says
You have to want it my dear
you have to force yourself
it's not enough if I wheel you
in front of the open window
and you breathe in the fresh air
that's not enough
you need a change of scenery
Believe me dear
I want what's best for you
(*The telephone rings off-stage.*
Vera exits.
Clara looks after her.)
VERA: (*Speaks off-stage, but she can't be understood. She returns with a striped inmate's jacket.*)
Rudolf
if everything is ready
he's on his way
(*Referring to the inmate's jacket.*)
Maybe he wants you
to put it on
it's possible
(*Hangs the SS trousers on the wall and irons the inmate's jacket.*)
Suddenly it may occur to him
that you should put it on

and he'll want me to shave your head
You'll ruin your eyes my dear
(*Walks over to Clara and turns a light on for her.*)
Come on give me the papers
Rudolf will be here any moment
He doesn't like you
reading those papers
(*Takes the stack of papers and exits.*)
Tomorrow morning you can read again
(*Clara examines the pair of socks which she mended.*)
VERA: (*Enters.*)
Once he's no longer at court
he'll be home all day
he isn't much of a walker as you know
he'll just sit around all day
and wait
(*Walks to the ironing board and holds the inmate's jacket up against the light.*)
Sometimes I think
he's much too good natured
Some of his sentences are much too lenient
he didn't make the best of our penal code
even though he had the opportunity
then again he can be so tough it's hard to understand
(*Exits with the inmate's jacket.*)
CLARA: (*Calling after her.*)
I won't put it on
even if he wants me to
not today
VERA: (*Enters with Rudolf's boots, sits down and polishes them.*)
Wait and see
how everything goes
we mustn't irritate him
you have to control yourself
If he wants you to
just put on the jacket
you've got to you know that
(*Gets up, takes the SS uniform from the wall and takes it out.*)
CLARA:
Not today
I can't
I won't
VERA: (*Comes back and continues to polish the boots.*)
It's just for tonight
let him have his fun
we all have our follies
But he is serious about it
deadly serious
(*Gets up, sits down in front of the mirror and combs her hair.*)

At first I thought
it's just a quirk
but then I realized that he is serious
about this birthday
I never resisted him
And what else could you do
but go along with it
after thirty years
it's too late to change anything
You know how Rudolf is
I am glad
that Justice Roesch won't be coming today
that we can be by ourelves
(*Turns toward Clara.*)
But for you the company of Justice Roesch
would mean a welcome distraction
(*Starts to braid one braid.*)
I can easily go back in time
(*Lifts up her head and looks in the mirror.*)
Of course I'm no longer the young maiden in braids
but he wants it this way
Why shouldn't I do what he wants
I must admit I think it's very nice of you
to go along
even though you hate it
I admire you

CLARA:
Now you look as you did forty years ago
but even forty years ago
I couldn't stand you
You always tortured me
you never missed an opportunity to torture me
as if all you ever did was devise
new ways to torture me
always new humiliations
like my father
wasn't really my father
you told me that one often
you lied to me
you humiliated me
whenever you could
At night when I slept and you didn't
you pulled me by my braids out of bed
You locked me in the cellar
you secretly tore up my clothes
(*Starts combing herself.*)
You started it with Rudolf didn't you

you took advantage of the situation
it's disgusting
VERA:
You simply don't know
what's going on inside a person
you don't even know what's going on inside yourself
you just keep nagging
and drag everything through the mud
What's between Rudolf and me
is completely clean it is pure
you should be hit every time you open your mouth
but you're my sister
it's not my fault that I can walk and you can't
I'm punished in other ways
(*Sticks out her tongue in front of the mirror.*)
It just happened this way
all you ever see is some plot against you
it's not immoral my dear
Good God the way you carry on
instead of being glad
you're not in pain
What if you were in pain all the time
There you sit and you're all right
you have every wish taken care of
but that you can't walk and run off
is something you can't blame on anyone
You see us as the guilty parties
Rudolf and myself that is
I can't drive this madness out of your head
What a good life you could have
if you could simply be content
Rudolf and I we suffer more from you than you suffer yourself
that's the truth
he is such a kindhearted man
who gives his all
and I too am I not at your disposal day and night
but you don't see that
you don't want to see that
although you know it very well
We hate those who help us
(*Works on her second braid.*)
The truth is that we sacrificed ourselves for you
We could have left
we didn't leave
so that you wouldn't be left alone
we could have sold this house

we didn't
for your sake
We could put you into an institution
then we would be by ourselves
how nice it would be sometimes
and how often do I wish
you were in an institution
and would leave me alone and in peace
Do you really believe Rudolf is happy
this is no constellation
to give happiness
to a man his age and in his position
Rudolf's life deserved quite another final chapter
we sacrificed it for you
(*Sticks out her tongue.*)
and all we get is your relentless hate
for myself and Rudolf
You are our enemy
not like someone of our own flesh and blood
Every cripple torments his nurse
father used to say
until they drop dead
In fact you are the strongest of us all
You will outlive us all
I am sure
you will outlive us all
How much longer can Rudolf go on
with his bad heart
You are the healthiest
that makes it even more grotesque
You control us
not the other way around
we are the ones who need help
not you
you determine what happens
whether I get to the theatre or not
You sit in your wheelchair as if it were a throne
and you give the orders
A bomb put you in first position
your immobility has paralyzed us
Rudolf and myself
I dread the day
he takes off his robe
never to put it on again
It is his retirement
I fear

then all three of us will be sitting here
in this room
just waiting to die
But who knows how long it will take
a process of gradual mortification
Then you will sit in judgment of us
that's what I'm afraid of
Rudolf of course suspects what lies ahead of him
but he doesn't have the strength to say it
(*Looks around.*)
How I hate all this furniture
I am never alone
I am under your constant surveillance
If I do go out it means rushing back home
to my poor sister
People will never know what it means
to be watched that closely
by someone like you
and to be judged
You deny me a heart
yet yours is cold as ice
(*Gets up, walks over to Clara and combs her hair.*)
How contradictory each of us is
how vicious we can be
combing you hair relaxes me
(*Gives the comb to Clara and walks back to the dresser, sits down if front of the mirror.*)
Your misery isn't just yours alone
it's our misery too
above all our misery
Once Rudolf is retired
things will change perhaps
We will travel
You'll see Rudolf will take you out
every day off to the park
into the city with Rudolf
Then he'll have the time to sit with you in the park
(*Pins her braids to her head.*)
He is a kind man
Everyone says so
Everyone who knows him knows how kind he is
All these insidious rumors
(*Exclaims.*)
And even what they say is true
it happened so long ago
I don't think Rudolf is guilty

of a crime
not he
(*Turns toward Clara and shows her her braids pinned to her head.*)
That's how he likes me
just like that
Do you remember
us running around this way as little girls
during the war
during the Nazis
(*Turns toward the mirror, looks into it and undoes her hairdo, untying her braids.*)
First Rudolf takes a bath
What if
Rudolf hadn't come back
if he had gone on under his own name
Ten years in the military underground
After that no one asked any more questions
Now they start dredging up the past again
hunting down every decent law-abiding citizen
(*Turns toward Clara.*)
Rudolf is a good good man
You are proof of it
What's past doesn't matter
And who's to know how it really was
Now they are digging up the dirt again
You should have seen
how the children loved him
they all love him
Kindness creates enemies
father used to say
During war there are no laws
father used to say
(*Listens.*)
Do you hear something
I thought it was Rudolf
If only he can make the transition
if only he doesn't fall apart
The Government automatically exiles
its most accomplished people into retirement
the best ones far too soon
But the Government can afford it right
Rudolf would love to stay in office
but no the authorities stick to the date of birth
and send him home
They never had a better judge
If only all judges were like him
How quickly time passes

it seems only yesterday
that Rudolf became Chief Justice
It's the most difficult
public office Rudolf says
the most responsible one
Being a judge means setting the perfect example
He always was the sickliest among us
do you remember
a cold every moment
and if he'd jumped out of a window just for the fun of it
you could be sure he'd land on a rusty tin
every other moment he'd be walking with a limp
or have to stay in bed
mother loved him
he was her favorite
she always took his side
(*Gets up and walks to the window. Takes the uniform from its hanger.*)
He is the only one
She'd paid attention to
without Rudolf we wouldn't be here anymore
(*Takes the clothes brush and brushes the uniform.*)
Rudolf has proven
who he really is
We know
and love our brother
He still is the child
he once was
(*Looks through the window.*)
the timid shy child
We must stick by him you understand
very very closely
(*Brushes the uniform.*)
he needs us
(*Looks through the pockets for something and finally pulls out the Iron Cross of the First Order.*)
Our hero
(*Pins the Iron Cross on the uniform jacket.*)
I beg you
don't cause any trouble
you've got to control yourself
for my sake
for our sake
promise me
maybe it is the last time
I always dread this day
He must celebrate this day

his own way you understand
you've got to control yourself
(*Looks through the window, suddenly:*)
Rudolf is here
How lucky everything is ready
I even got the azaleas
Rudolf's favorite flowers
(*Exits with the uniform.*)

Curtain.

ACT II

Ten minutes later.
Rudolf in his chair, exhausted.
Clara mending Rudolf's socks.
Vera enters with Rudolf's winter coat.

RUDOLF:
   Here's the button here
   (*Searches his jacket for his button and finally finds it.*)
   There
   They tried to stop me again
   near the school
   as I was passing by with Roesch
VERA:
   Those Jew boys
RUDOLF:
   I'll have a talk with their father some time
   I'm sure Mr. Schwartz is behind all this
   always the same place
   (*To Clara.*)
   Now the Jew boys are hanging out
   where your tragedy occurred
   If you hadn't been in school that day
   everything would have been different
   Right on target smack into the school
   And only two days before the end
VERA:
   Schwartz of all people
   Who do they think they are
   that they can carry on like that
   (*Rudolf gives Vera the button to his coat and Vera fixes the button.*)
   I'll be glad when you are retired Rudolf
   Then all these troubles will be over

But maybe those kids were just playing
RUDOLF:
Today of all days
There is a connection
between today's date
and the way those youngsters came at me
VERA:
Maybe it's just your imagination
Mr. Schwartz always treats me very kindly
I always get the best service in his shop
RUDOLF:
Maybe you're right
maybe it is just my imagination
I am a little exhausted that's true
But why me of all people
They didn't go after Roesch
A year ago they stopped me
at the very same place
VERA:
They're just children Rudolf
they don't know what they're doing
Unruly undisciplined like everyone else nowadays
Everything's changed
children nowadays can do as they please
Besides at our age we just can't take children anymore
You would have never put up with children
What a thought you and children
(*Has fixed the button and bites off the thread.*)
We were still brought up well
Today's children grow up like savages
This descent into barbarity comes from America
Savage children are ruling the world today
There's nothing but chaos all around
(*Rudolf gets up, gets into his coat. Vera is helping him.*)
VERA:
Where will it all end
with everyone heading toward chaos
RUDOLF: (*Buttoning his coat.*)
I've been wearing this coat for ten years
I should have a new one made
But not before I retire
Ten years in the same coat
You won't find that among my colleagues
(*Goes to the window, looks out.*)
There they're suddenly pushing me around

pulling on me and the button is off
(Takes off the coat again.)
There is a connection between all this
VERA:
You are overworked Rudolf that's all
you overdid it lately
All this devotion to duty
and who thanks you for it
I'll be glad when everything is over
As Chief Justice you get a handsome pension
then we won't have to give a damn
then all we care about is ourselves
RUDOLF: *(Gives the coat back to Vera and sits down.)*
We have no reason to complain of course
Things could have been quite different
Everyone has his own cross to bear
(To Clara.)
Our victim how is she today
are you in pain
All day I'm haunted by the thought of you
sitting at home in pain
Just think though
soon we'll be going to Egypt
all three of us
(To Vera.)
We'll pack up and go
to Genoa and from there by boat
to Alexandria
I've been dreaming about this for decades
I can hardly wait
(Gets up and goes toward Clara.)
You shall always have a good life my dear
We can consider ourselves lucky
Others have turned to dust years ago
(Walks to the window and looks out.)
The factory was voted down
I got it through
It certainly would be unbearable
to have a factory wall in front of our window
VERA:
Now see how influential you are
You only have to want something
and you get it
RUDOLF:
Now they'll build it on the other side of town
it won't bother us there

What a depressing view it would be
Instead of trees
we would see a wall
behind which they manufacture poison
(*To Clara.*)
For your sake I put up a fight
against the construction of that plant
The decision came this morning at eleven
VERA:
Oh Rudolf we have to celebrate this too
RUDOLF:
Of course I made a lot of enemies
VERA:
They can't harm you anymore
You've achieved everything you ever wanted
RUDOLF:
Destroying nature
cutting down trees
cutting down those beautiful old trees
for the sake of a chemical plant
which produces nothing but poison
The profit mongers get their hands on everything
The world has never been so brutal
profit guides and governs everything
Wherever some land has still been preserved
you can be sure that industry moves in
But not here I told them
not here
not in front of my window
where nature is still untouched
I love our view
CLARA:
But you can't see a thing
RUDOLF:
Not now
but that doesn't alter the fact that this view
is my favorite view
When the fog is gone
even in winter when the branches are all ice
and all is white like made of glass
(*Turns around and goes toward Clara.*)
Roesch asked me
why we didn't put you in an institution
But I told him
the thought never entered our minds
having you institutionalized
We and that means Vera and I and you

we shall stay together
no matter how long
I swore to it
We must endure one another my child
It will all be better once I'm at home
then I can take on some of Vera's work
we can go to the park every day
and into town twice a week maybe
Your brother likes to see you happy
Once I'm no longer in office
I'll be free
and that means all three of us will be free
(*Goes to Vera.*)
Now I often think
it is time to quit
it really is too much for me
then again when I look at Roesch
married
(*Sits down.*)
two children
what you might call a family
he's not as fit as I
yet he's much younger
Family life burns you out very quickly
we've managed fairly well
we can't complain
Luckily the house is paid off
now we have our peace
Marriage is something horrible
people run into it blindly
craving this marital bliss
they can hardly wait for it
at seventeen or eighteen that soon
they make their child
and get married
We've had it better the three of us
A higher level of consciousness
(*Vera sits down.*)
A higher degree of difficulty
not without its troubles of course
not without despair as father used to say
Things were just the way they were that's all
(*To Clara who had put away the socks and is reading a book now.*)
If you hadn't been wrecked
and you'll forgive me such harsh words
you would have married
you would be gone

to who knows where
in any case you would have married
living your own life
but most likely you wouldn't even be alive
you would have destroyed yourself
your tragedy saved you from destruction
the bomb that hit the school
only as a cripple
did you have a chance to survive
(*Facing Vera.*)
am I not right
this is how we became what we are
a conspiracy against the stupidity of life
(*Looks at Clara.*)
She pretends to read
one of her books of lies
and she despises us
(*To Vera.*)
We all deserve what we are
(*Looks at the watch.*)
Six o'clock
(*Vera gets up and goes to the piano.*)
RUDOLF: (*To Clara.*)
That's a good idea
play something
I haven't heard you play in a long time
maybe you can't anymore
it's been so long
In the old days music used to count so much
(*Vera starts to play. She improvises on "A Little Night Music" by Mozart.*)
RUDOLF: (*To Clara.*)
I used to love it
when she sat down and played
at twilight
like old times
When I lived in hiding
behing closed curtains
during my cellar days
I'd venture upstairs around nine at night
and listen to her
that's when she'd play for me
And you'd sit exactly where you're sitting now
and watch me
You hated me then as you hate me now
I got used to it
I got tough just like you
we all got tough

For ten years I had to hide
then it was time
to see the daylight again
Who would have thought
that I would end my career as Chief Justice
and retire with an enormous pension
(*Looks at Vera.*)
Who would have thought so Vera
That's how times change
At first ten years hidden in a cellar
hidden by you and Clara
And then suddenly this rise
I have no bad conscience
Now and then things get a bit sticky for me
that's true even today
but I don't have a bad conscience
if that were the case all the others
would have to feel much worse than I
I only did my duty
and I paid my dues
I did my work and I accomplished more
than could be expected of me
I paid my dues
I owe no apologies
(*Turns around.*)
On this day the seventh of October a day of reckoning
I swore
to go through with it my way
(*To Clara.*)
You always find it quite repulsive
but to me it's a necessity
to Vera too it's a necesity
and we do celebrate this birthday
in all due modesty
just the three of us in the quiet of our home
If it weren't for Himmler
this house wouldn't be here
you know what would be here instead
a poison plant
isn't it strange Vera that today
I too could prevent
the construction of a toxic gas plant
right in front of our windows
Forty years ago Himmler prevented it
today I prevented it
There's no such thing as coincidence
If I could have said in front of the city council

what was really on my mind
when the city council rejected the project
Of course I had to hold my tongue
I exercised my power
I really did
categorically
and maybe for the last time
His Honor the Chief Justice showed his muscle
his word counts
they all listened to me
they all accepted my arguments
now of course I have the other part of town
against me
Once they start construction work there
But in our part of town which is prettier more valuable
they'll thank me forever
In a hundred years hence
when we won't even be alive anymore
They will still talk about this council meeting
the one in which Chief Justice Hoeller
was able to have the final word
saving this district from the worst possible fate

VERA:
You are really enjoying this
You really are in your element
and today of all days

RUDOLF:
What a coincidence
which it isn't
that today of all days was the day of the meeting
and that a decision was reached
People don't even realize
how much they owe me
For generations to come
I saved nature in this district

VERA:
Oh Rudolf one day they'll build you
a monument a real statue

RUDOLF:
I couldn't have done any more
(*Looks toward Clara.*)
Yet I kept only thinking of us
how we must not let them destroy
the view from our window
this barbarous industrial society
that already destroyed ninety percent of our globe

The war bred its own kind of profiteers
but peace time wheeler-dealers are much worse
The Jews destroy annihilate the surface of the earth
and some day they will have achieved
its final destruction
The Jews sell out nature
Democracy is a fraud
But woe to the man who raises his voice these days
to give away such truths
they cut his throat no less
(*Looks at Clara.*)
But it's obvious of course
that the exceptions prove the rule
and I myself met hundreds and thousands
of decent Jews
I'm not talking about those
I'm talking about the criminal ones
it's the ruthless Jew I'm talking about
who under the guise of democracy
exploits nature and wrecks the earth
unscrupulously
(*Vera closes the piano.*)
We are living in terrible times
we Europeans did everything wrong
once this is understood it will be too late
Americanism has poisoned us
Those who glorify democracy
are in fact its murderers
But we live in a thoroughly opportunistic world
which only knows the language of hypocrisy
not one truthful word is spoken by anyone
thus we are heading toward a dreadful situation
(*Gets up, goes to the window and looks out.*)
The worst degeneration has affected
all walks of life
Sometimes I wish I were no longer alive
when it's this gray and cold outside
and there is no one I can openly talk to
always functioning with a paralyzed tongue
filled with lies and shameless through and through
We'd be living in totally different times
had we been able to have it our way
Things will be different again mark my words
but we won't live to see it
the young will wake up
and not stand for what's happening now
VERA: (*Goes to Rudolf.*)
Why rack your brains

it won't do any good
but of course this day
makes you think this way
We are doing all right
no one is bothering us really
(*Kisses his forehead.*)
Just think what you are
and who you are
None of this filth can harm you

RUDOLF:
One day the Germans will realize
what the Americans did to them

VERA:
We will have a nice party
and no one can stop us
no one
(*Turns toward Clara.*)

RUDOLF: (*Also facing Clara.*)
We shall win
the enemy will destroy itself

VERA: (*Takes both of Rudolf's hands and leads him back to the chair at the window. They both sit down.*)
I'm proud of you
of what you accomplished today
Chief Justice Hoeller
kept the toxic gas plant away from our window

RUDOLF:
I knew of course
that the crucial meeting was to be on October seventh
I staked all my bets on one deal
I was a one man conspiracy against all
for the prevention of this plant
first most of the votes were against me
but then I felt
the force of my arguments coming through
and soon the majority of the votes were on my side
even Roesch initially against me
finally voted down the construction of the plant
in this spot
with the meeting still in session I crossed the room
and thanked him
I even convinced the Socialists

VERA:
Now you are the old Rudolf again
whom I always admired
whom I love

(*To Clara, while she is holding Rudolf's wrist.*)
Isn't it true
Rudolf is his old self again
strong willed unbending tough
The road we walked on
was strewn with many stones
but now it is clear
Every man's goodness
will assert itself one day
and you are a good man Rudolf
(*With a glance at Clara.*)
we know it
Often it was tough going
You took completely after father
if he could see
what you've achieved
He had to die so soon
before he could have the slightest idea
of what would become of you
RUDOLF:
I owe you two so much
VERA:
It's your own energy Rudolf
Because you never gave in
and because you paid no attention
to other people's opinions
God forbid you had listened to them
you would have perished
they would have trampled you to death
(*Rudolf stretches out his legs and Vera takes off his shoes.*)
VERA:
It's just awful to think
that they might have had it their way
had they discovered your hiding place
For almost ten years you didn't venture
into the streets
It's a disgrace for our country
(*Looks at his feet.*)
Your feet are swollen Rudolf
Soon all this standing in the cold court room will be over
Everything there is inhuman
What was going on today
RUDOLF:
The Meissner murder case
A cold blooded individual
Everything was clear from the beginning

      but the Law demands
      that we deal with such animals
      for over half a year
      What's the use of a lifetime sentence
      if after fifteen years these people
      are on the loose again
VERA:
      One really lives in constant fear
      (*With a glance at Clara.*)
      Clara mended your socks
      Five pairs today
      she works hard
      I use these woollen socks to trick her
      into forgetting about her reading
      Every day a dozen papers
      plus the books
      The money it costs
      But that's not even the point
      She already has
      a thoroughly twisted mind
      What it took me today of all days
      to keep her
      away from her papers
      I simply snatched them away from her
      As soon as she is done with her mending
      her head's back in the books again
RUDOLF:
      And to what papers did you write today
      Your letters to the editor always
      exaggerate
      because you write so many
      nobody takes you seriously any more
VERA: She got herself hopelessly stuck
      in this political fanaticism
      we must consider our sister a lost case
      Just imagine us without our enemy
      (*Takes off Rudolf's socks.*)
      It will be good
      when you're no longer in office
      My dear Chief Justice
RUDOLF: (*Takes off his jacket. Vera helps him.*)
      It's much too hot in here
VERA: (*Who has helped him into a pair of slippers.*)
      I keep it that way for Clara
      all she does is sit in her wheelchair
      and read all day

RUDOLF:
> But it's not healthy
> in such overheated rooms
> (*Vera gets up and opens the window.*)
> I shall spend much time out in nature
> and I will pursue my music again
> You can get my violin ready
> get the dust off
> Do you think I still can play it

VERA:
> It's something you don't forget Rudolf
> not a master like you

RUDOLF:
> It won't click anymore

VERA:
> Nobody ever played the violin as well as you
> a born virtuoso that's what you are

RUDOLF:
> I can't even read music anymore

VERA: She got herself hopelessly stuck
> in this political fanaticism
> we must consider our sister a lost case
> Just imagine us without our enemy
> (*Takes off Rudolf's socks.*)
> It will be good
> when you're no longer in office
> My dear Chief Justice

RUDOLF: (*Takes off his jacket. Vera helps him.*)
> It's much too hot in here

VERA: (*Who has helped him into a pair of slippers.*)
> I keep it that way for Clara
> all she does is sit in her wheelchair
> and read all day

RUDOLF:
> But it's not healthy
> in such overheated rooms
> (*Vera gets up and opens the window.*)
> I shall spend much time out in nature
> and I will pursue my music again
> You can get my violin ready
> get the dust off
> Do you think I still can play it

VERA:
> It's something you don't forget Rudolf
> not a master like you

RUDOLF:
> It won't click anymore

VERA:
   Nobody ever played the violin as well as you
   a born virtuoso that's what you are
RUDOLF:
   I can't even read music anymore
VERA:
   In your sleep you can
RUDOLF:
   In my sleep
   The things we can do in our sleep
   We can hardly believe
   all the things we can do in our sleep
   Without music it's so empty here
   don't you agree
   (*Takes off his vest, slips down his suspenders with a glance at Clara.*)
   I'm not appreciated
   sitting around like this I know
   but I can't stand it any other way
   where else but at home
   can I let myself go
VERA:
   All day long the severest discipline
RUDOLF:
   Mask of dignity over my face
   his Honor the Chief Justice
   You have no idea
   how impertinent people are nowadays
   how shrewd
   (*Takes a deep breath.*)
   No we must hold together
   it won't be easy
   (*Looks at the ceiling.*)
   Then we'll have the place painted
   and perhaps the furniture rearranged
   maybe the dresser here
   and the two chairs over there
   The piano should be more in the light
   And different curtains
   these were already our grandparents'
VERA:
   Yes how well they used to make things
   they last and last
   The things they're making now
   are worthless
   by the time one gets used to them
   they're already falling apart

RUDOLF:
　　Let them build their plant in this district
　　I said
　　I said it very loudly very clearly
　　but then you'll have destroyed
　　the face of this town our home town
　　utterly
　　forever
　　just for a momentary profit's sake
　　Then there was a pause
　　Then I spoke about
　　what this district means to our town
　　what it's always meant to me
　　one must get personal if one wants to convince
　　I described a few childhood impressions
　　this and that from our childhood
　　how we used to play in the park with our parents
　　such happy parents such happy children
　　I said
　　You are destroying all that
　　if you vote for the plant
　　the whole town will be wrecked
　　Think it over think what you're doing
　　Then they voted against the plant
VERA:
　　Oh Rudolf isn't it nice
　　such agreement
　　such solidarity
　　(*Gets up and kisses his forehead.*)
　　They know what they have in you
　　(*Leaves with the shoes.*)
RUDOLF: (*To Clara.*)
　　Every now and then
　　the thinking man has the obligation
　　to intervene in world affairs
　　and even if it is only
　　to prevent a gas plant in a place
　　where it doesn't belong
VERA: (*Enters with Himmler's photograph.*)
　　You see I got a new frame for the Reichsfuehrer SS
　　that's my gift for this day
　　for Himmler's birthday
　　solid silver
　　come on take it
　　(*Rudolf takes the photograph.*)
　　If the jeweler had only known

what picture was going in that frame
Do you like it
RUDOLF:
Very precious very precious
VERA:
I had to look for a long time
to find just the frame
(*Takes the picture and leaves again.*)
RUDOLF: (*To Clara.*)
You are so considerate
As one grows older and older
one gets more considerate
(*Vera enters and sits down.*)
Incidentally I met Doctor Fromm
(*To Clara.*)
he asked about you
I told him you were fine
no complications whatsoever
he still thinks
you should be institutionalized
However I assured him
that we are determined
to never have you institutionalized
even though all things considered
that's what I said
it might be better for your health
there's nothing we can do for you in medical terms
I said that yes
since this is October seventh after all
I didn't mention that
but I thought so to myself
if the Americans hadn't attacked the school
Two days before the war was over
innocent people
this poor helpless child I said
I called it a terror attack
but he didn't react to that
Ninety-two dead children I said and he
What ninety-two
I completely forgot
Yes said I
one easily forgets these horrible figures
If my sister Clara
the most intelligent of us I said to him
had not been struck by that falling beam
Oh yes of course said Doctor Fromm that beam

A terror attack just two days before the end I said
Wouldn't he like to visit us
not for medical purposes I said
medically speaking he has no business in our house
for a chat I said
my two sisters Vera and Clara would certainly be pleased
a man with such extraordinary abilities
such knowledge
with so profound an education
and so charming I said
he took his leave
he was clearly upset because
I spoke of a terror attack
that shows right away he's a Jew
Medical people are a strange breed
I never got along with them
You ask them something
they talk around the answer
they can't look you in the face
Doctors have had a bad conscience
for centuries father said
he was right
If you beilieve a doctor you are lost
father used to say
getting involved with a doctor
means getting involved with death no less
If we put ourselves in the hands of doctors
we are doomed to death
If we happen to run into a doctor
it's best to turn the other way
and we will save ourselves from horrendous lifelong ailments
and in most cases we'll even escape death itself
Doctors are death's delivery boys father said
Of course if we only use them for our own purposes
to have them at our command as it were
to cut out an appendix or cut off a leg
since otherwise we would kick off anyway
but otherwise
the company of doctors is the most dangerous
you do better as our father said
inviting the first violinist of the Philharmonic Orchestra
that can't do any harm
if we only do it once or twice a year
And you know what he said
our Doctor Fromm
before he took off

and after I conversed with him
in the most civilized manner
Weren't you substitute camp commander
he put special emphasis on substitute
before I realized what he meant
he was off and away
People have started
to dig up the past again
something's been set in motion
it's not hard to guess by whom
it's a good thing we cut off all social contacts
we don't need anybody
VERA:
Oh Rudolf nothing can happen to you
ten years in a cellar that's something
way down there with the rats
RUDOLF: (*With a glance at Clara.*)
I can imagine what's going on inside your sister Clara
but let's leave it at that
The fact is that we did everything humanly possible
for our country
that we spent our lives breaking our backs
for its people
corrosion and destruction are the result
but it will change
Something is brewing
in our favor
people can't fool me
most of them are good Germans
who want no part
in what is going on today
The good German detests what's going on in this country
Depravity hypocrisy general stupefaction
The Jewish element has taken root everywhere
again you can see it everywhere in every nook and cranny
VERA:
Oh Rudolf
You must take it easy
you must take care of yourself
RUDOLF:
There is a criminal in each of us
he just has to be called upon
that's how it has always been
that's how it will always be
(*Takes a handkerchief from his trousers, wipes his forehead, and points outside with his handkerchief.*)

There right there
an enormous wall
behind which poison is produced
poison to exterminate insects
gas
VERA:
Today's a big day for you
the day you prevented an enormous disaster
RUDOLF:
It is inconceivable
right on this beautiful piece of land
Industry has the main say
industry not democracy
Democracy is the biggest nonsense
that ever existed
Democracy is the biggest business for those
in charge of democracy
(*To Clara.*)
Speechless as always
VERA: (*Sits down.*)
And merciless
From her vantage point she watches us and waits
until the day she'll strike out
RUDOLF: (*Jumping up, angrily.*)
Where do you get all your hate you and your kind
who gives you the right
VERA: (*Calming him down.*)
Sit down Rudolf sit down
(*Rudolf sits down.*)
VERA:
It's just a game
it's nothing serious
it can't be serious
It's a real comedy
sometimes we forget that
Why shouldn't we play this comedy
especially today
I admire you Clara
she plays the hardest part
We only give her the cues
With her speechlessness
she keeps the comedy in motion
RUDOLF:
Now the office is beginning
to get to me
We used to say we're getting old

and now we already are
(*Vera starts to massage his neck first and then his whole back.*)
One thing is sure
there's no one you can trust
they're all spies
Follow your distrust
father said
All life long alone
everyone by himself
And all for what
Sometimes I think it were better
to have died in Siberia
like our nephew
instead of having gone through all this
how strenuous it is
how it's dragging on
we have to live and don't even want to
for the few hours we can count on one hand
Where did we get all that energy
If I had taken up music
or mathematics
But that's not for a lawyer's son
(*Recoils from pain.*)
VERA:
Here it is
RUDOLF:
Yes right in that spot
After three o'clock my whole body aches
but this feels good
(*Vera opens his shirt and massages him lower down.*)
If you had married taken a husband
most likely a lawyer whom else
with a fortune
from a wealthy family
had you moved into a modern house
had children
you'd still be alone now
old age leaves everyone alone
first they have children so that they won't be alone
and then they are completely alone
I can see them all around me
growing old and lonely
what's left to a man is him alone
and old
VERA:
Whom could I have married

    I can't think of one man
    You maybe
RUDOLF:
    If I hadn't been around
    if circumstances hadn't been what they were
    Didn't you have to come down to the cellar
    and take care of me
    And of Clara
    You are a brave girl Vera
    how different from your mother
    you made it through everything
    she quit
    a tiny breeze and she was gone
    (*Vera wants to take off his shirt, but in order to do so, he has to unbutton his pants.*)
    You are the bravest of us all
    the most dependable one
    First they couldn't find me
    because you were hiding me
    then the dust could settle
    for ten years
    and then it all happened very quickly
    (*Now Vera takes off his shirt completely and puts it on his shoulders.*)
    I grew into my office as they say
    a man takes on the features of his office
    he merges with his office
    I had no other choice
    whatever I did I was forced to do
    and I did nothing
    I couldn't justify
    on the contrary
VERA:
    You are racking your brains
    for no reason at all
    All those people digging up the past
    totally incompetent
    He who acts in good faith and conscience
    shall prevail in the end father said
RUDOLF:
    I have no bad conscience
VERA:
    Of course not
    One day you will be able to speak openly
    about everything you have to keep silent about now
    The time will come sooner than you think
RUDOLF:
    If it can be arranged

    we will go to sea
    to Egypt of course
    that's what I've always missed
    a cultural excursion
    back to antiquity
    the pyramids
    Persepolis
    we are all victims of the war
    A life dear Vera
    utterly devoted to the penal code
    You should have seen that bastard
    at the scene of the crime
    cold to the bone
    cynical
    complete indifference toward his victim
    killing a man for four thousand
    but they are all alike
    that didn't exist in our days
    such elements simply didn't exist
    they never surfaced to begin with
    each trial opens your eyes
    to a human cesspool
    now I'm just about sick of it
VERA:
    Only a few more months
    and it will all be over
RUDOLF:
    Actually I'm glad
    When I think that
    fifteen years after I retire
    people will still be sitting out their sentences
    the ones I passed upon them
    I won't even be alive for that
    How one can be a judge
    father used to say
    I ask myself how one can be a judge
    a curse hangs over this office
VERA:
    Oh Rudolf you are overtired
    You take your bath
    and everything will look quite different
    We'll have a good dinner tonight
    The champagne is chilled
    I've got everything ready for you
    the way you've always wanted it
    everything the way you're used to it

everything brushed and ironed
boots polished
by me not by Olga
RUDOLF:
Substitute commander he said
substitute camp commander
so young and already a judge
In principle I never had anything against the Jews
We always had our Jewish friends
VERA:
Once you're in retirememt
I'll get slip covers for these chairs
don't you think they're pretty shabby
Our mother had them upholstered
We changed absolutely nothing in here
everything is the way we took it over from our parents
Out of piety you always said
we won't change anything
And new curtains
We should change everything just a bit
once you're out of office
who cares about the money
for decades we never indulged
in any kind of luxury
always frugal
Everything for Clara
nothing for us
(*Kneels down in front of him and starts massaging his feet.*)
I wouldn't do this for anyone else
for no other man but you
The majority is on our side you know that
Her husband was with the Military SS
Mrs. Leupold said
and then she showed me her living room
Come on in it's all right she said
you see this is where my husband rejuvenates
this is his temple
nothing but memorabilia from his military days
Iron Crosses handwritten documents
by the highest dignitaries of our time
You are my hero my baby
you needn't be afraid
Afraid of what
(*Looks at Clara.*)
If she could talk
if she could walk out of here

and talk
if she weren't dependent on us
she would betray us
if it didn't mean her death
this is how we all pay our dues
in order to maintain
the balance of our conspiracy
yes there was something else Mrs. Leupold had
she opened several drawers
and showed me this and that belonging to her husband
medals and pieces of clothing
several pieces of jewelry from Jews
She had known for a long time
that we shared the same views
but I mustn't tell anyone
what I had seen there
her husband made her swear
but she showed me everything
she even has a letter from the Fuehrer
but that letter's locked up in a safe
Her husband has dealings with the Near East
Business isn't bad
One of his nieces fell off a horse
and for twenty years
she's been a paraplegic just like Clara
they put her in an institution in the Black Forest
she's doing well there
they have the best doctors
(*The telephone rings in the adjoining room.*)
RUDOLF:
Who can that be
No one calls on October seventh
VERA:
Wait
(*Exits.*)
RUDOLF: (*To Clara.*)
Who can that be
(*Vera can be heard talking, but she can't be understood.*)
RUDOLF:
I think it is Roesch
CLARA:
That disgusting man
RUDOLF:
He saved my life
CLARA:
He saved your life

If only he hadn't saved your life
If only he hadn't saved you
All our misery comes from him
saving your life
What a life
If he hadn't dragged you out of the fire
we too would have perished
But this way you came back
and caused all our misery
RUDOLF:
The way you talk to me
Too much
CLARA:
He should have let you burn
RUDOLF:
Is this the thanks
for what I did for you
which is everything I could possibly do
CLARA:
For what you did
did
did
It would have been so simple
if you hadn't come back
I was terrified
when you appeared
I sensed this was my tragedy
That's why I hate that man
your friend and partisan
You two make me sick
I hate you two
I always hated the two of you
You ruthlessness
your hypocrisy
your viciousness
RUDOLF:
I have to take this
from a cripple
who spends her time
stuffing her head with printed garbage
with demented freakish ideas
with perverted literature
which I abhor
CLARA:
I abhor you
you and everything you do
everything you ever did

    and I abhor Vera
RUDOLF:
    We should have left you on your own
    then nothing would be left of you
    You would be dead gone finished
CLARA:
    That's your language all right
    that is the language of the judge
    the Chief of Justice
RUDOLF:
    Look who's talking
    in our time we simply put the likes of you
    under gas
CLARA:
    You oh yes your kind oh yes
    You constantly talk about the scum
    and what are you
VERA: (*Enters. Clara pretends she is reading.*)
    Roesch
    it was him
    he is sorry he couldn't come
    I turned off the telephone
    He has a cold
    he wanted to call the doctor
    but then he changed his mind
    he is with us all the way he said
RUDOLF:
    He saved my life
    it would have been all over
    he pulled me out of the fire
    at the very last moment
VERA:
    What's the matter with you
    you're all upset
    What's going on
    (*Looks at Clara.*)
    What is it with you two
RUDOLF:
    She turned into a beast
    in her wheelchair
    a filthy rotten beast
VERA:
    Rudolf
RUDOLF:
    One shouldn't pay that much attention to her words
    she's demented
    perverted and demented

did we need this
having saved her
having kept her here
(*Vera massages Rudolf's neck.*)
If I hadn't come back
you may not have survived at all
VERA:
What makes you say that
RUDOLF:
For decades nothing but work just for her
and for you
day in day out
I paid my dues
If it weren't for you
(*Screams at Clara.*)
What an insult
what an insult
VERA:
What's the matter with you two
RUDOLF:
She keeps watching us
and waits only for the opportunity
to destroy us
that's all she's preparing for
(*To Clara.*)
but you won't make it
people like you
who squat in their wheelchairs for decades
fall over suddenly and drop dead
I don't hear of anyone getting very old
That's not what we deserved
I would be happy with Vera alone
happy happy happy
(*Points at Clara.*)
There squats our enemy
and waits
(*Jumps up.*)
Let me tell you Clara
I wish you'd drop dead
and leave us alone
you've tormented us for twenty years
even longer than that you've tormented us
But this is it now
this is it
Now it is
(*Sits down in the chair exhausted.*)
VERA:
Just leave her be

it's always the same
you two will never change
(*Kisses Rudolf on the forehead.*)
You are cold all over
come on get up
your bath is ready
everything is ready
my dear Rudolf
(*Rudolf gets up again. She embraces and kisses him, then Vera to Clara accusingly.*)
We belong together
Rudolf and I
we won't let you come between us

Curtain.

ACT III

The adjoining room.
Two hours later.
A dining table, chairs, easy chairs, a sofa, a cabinet with guns and a bureau.
Rudolf is slightly drunk, he is dressed in full uniform of a SS Obersturmbannfuehrer
with a gun in his belt and black knee-high boots.
Vera across from him, with her hair braided, wearing a long brocade gown.
Clara in her wheelchair, as before, positioned between them.
All three are eating and drinking champagne.

VERA:
    And then you'll come with us
    to the symphony Rudolf
    Of course we'll take Clara along
    It'll do her good to get out again
    (*Refills everybody's glasses.*)
    If it weren't for these occasional cultural pleasures
    what would life be without music
    People with culture father used to say
    If you're out of touch with the arts for too long
    You're bound to deteriorate
    Now I have to check
    if everything is safely locked
    (*Gets up and checks all doors and windows.*)
    One never knows
    Suddenly someone pops up
    A spy
    (*To Rudolf.*)
    You look so fine
    in that uniform
    it's a pity I always have to wait a whole year
    until you can put it on again
    nothing fits you quite so well
    Don't you think so Clara

(Clara is silent.)
And those beautiful medals on your chest
you are the true German Rudolf
The ideal
And you have to hide to put on that uniform
and hide to wear those medals
(Sits down again.)
If only I could go out with you
the way you look now
out of this house into town
to the opera center box
Oh Rudolf will we live to see that day
I don't think it will take too long
until we can openly confess to what we are
until justice returns
to the world once again
you say it yourself we live in a time
that's filled with injustice
You as a judge as the Chief Justice
(She takes off Rudolf's cap and puts it on the table.)
It's a shame
But the good and righteous shall prevail in the end
In this regard I trust father completely
(Lifts up her glass.)
Come Rudolf let's drink to your retirement
(To Clara.)
You too lift up your glass to our future
(To Rudolf.)
I am so looking forward to the day
you will be staying home for the very first time
(All three lift up their glasses and drink. Vera refills all glasses immediately.)
It's really admirable
the way you keep your oath
not letting them get to you
We must not be slaves
we must be free yes
You have my promise Rudolf
that I shall always be by your side
come what may
I've already proven it
in the darkest of times as you know
I paid my dues
as all of us did
To have an ideal and remain loyal to it
to always hold it dear and high
how beautiful
(To Clara.)

Those fine fillets of veal
I picked them especially for you
and now you don't even touch them
(*Holds a platter up for Clara, but Clara doesn't take anything, puts the platter back on the table. To Rudolf.*)
The tragedy is as father used to say
that against all better judgment
mankind always chooses the wrong path
Mankind is a patient
swallowing whatever is prescribed for him
every deathly poison father said
Rudolf you've kept your figure
for ten or twelve years now
the uniform fits you like the very first day you wore it
absolutely perfect
I am proud of you
His Honor the Chief Justice
and State Representative
If only I could have been there
when you were giving your speech
against the plant
You are a good speaker Rudolf
You convince when you speak
so impressively so clearly so convincingly
My dear State Representative
(*Gets up and adjusts the Iron Cross.*)
I pinned it too high
There now see
now it's in its proper place
(*Examines the Iron Cross and sits down again.*)
If we had to leave this place
because of that plant
Corporations always win
For the first time you really showed them
you singlehandedly
against a huge corporation
If only this could set a trend
But the politicians and the industrialists
are in league with one another
and slowly they ruin everything
polluting the air and wrecking it all
Pretty soon you won't even find a place in the Alps
to catch a breath of fresh clean air
Perhaps in Greenland
RUDOLF:
Perhaps in Greenland
you are absolutely right

Industry always controlled everything
I have nothing against industry
VERA:
Of course not
but in this case
When I think
that they might have built a plant here
we would have had to move
and give up everything
everything we cherish
Oh no
as long as we live
we won't leave this place
Here is our life
Here were our parents
here we were children
here we've made it
here is where we want to stay
RUDOLF:
And wait for the end
VERA:
Now now Rudolf
why so gloomy
You have no reason at all
You should be the happiest person alive
Wait
(*Gets up and gets a rather large photo album from the bureau. Sits down with it next to Rudolf, makes some room on the table for the album. To Clara.*)
You don't mind do you
if we look through our album
Remembering
once a year
Nothing like memories
What a beautiful album this is
Mother gave it to me
Christmas of thirty-nine
(*To Rudolf.*)
When you volunteered for the army
What a time
(*Turns a page.*)
Christmas thirty-nine
(*To Clara.*)
That's when you wore the Swiss dress Clara
how well it fit you that Swiss dress
which father brought you from his trip to Zurich
He promised
he would take us to Switzerland

yes you my dear children he said
to lake Zug
It didn't work out of course
(*Turns a page.*)
Seebruck do you remember Rudolf
we just returned from picking raspberries
(*To Rudolf.*)
You were always so ambitious
You always picked twice as many as I did
and Clara always ate them all
Uncle Rudolf took the picture
There you see the Kampen cliff
father climbed it to the top
He and his mountains
Father was a mountain man
Mother loved the sea the Adriatic sea
So they never vacationed together
because he always wanted the mountains
and she wanted the sea
(*Turns a page.*)
Uncle Rudolf went to the front
to Poland
terrible
(*To Clara.*)
Do you remember when uncle Rudolf was laid out
how afraid we were
terrified
we'd never seen a dead man before
Hardly half a year after he joined up
(*To Rudolf.*)
You bear a great resemblance to uncle Rudolf
The mouth the nose
from mother
The Poles were ruthless
always in ambush
At that time dead officers were still sent home
I cried for two days
(*Turns a page.*)
Pentecost in Vienna
Oh what a lovely time that was
the only trip we made with our parents
the only real trip
(*To Clara.*)
They let us ride on the big ferris wheel
You were afraid
and all of us went to the Hotel Sacher
and ate Sacher Torte

you didn't like it
(*Turns a page.*)
The first picture of you in your uniform
We were so proud of you
I kept bragging everywhere
that you are wearing the uniform now
Then off you were to Russia right away
a secret mission to the Russian front
for two months we didn't hear a thing
(*Turns a page.*)
The camp
how pretty those trees how pretty
And back there were your quarters right
What lovely countryside
And there you swam in the Weichsel river
(*To Clara.*)
Rudolf didn't have his belly then
not even a trace of a belly
The picture of the sailors
that was in Zoppot
That's were you went on vacation
and there you met Himmler
(*Turns a page.*)
And that is the picture
Roesch took of you and Himmler
Yes
Surely he didn't have to kill himself
he could have disappeared into safety
An act of panic
See now he thought of you
he gave you the forged passport you and Roesch

RUDOLF:
But of course it was also a consequence
he was basically a very sensitive human being
Nature simply does what it wants
father used to say
(*Stretches his legs under the table.*)
How nice it is
spending this day with you
quietly
without a sound coming through from outside
no noise nothing from outside
Being with you
joined in thoughts of our memories
(*Vera goes to the bureau and pushes the button of a tape recorder on top of the bureau. Beethoven's "Fifth."*)

RUDOLF: (*Closing his eyes.*)
Not so loud
softer my dear

(*Vera turns down the music.*)
No one can determine the course of his life
You're born and you die
everything in between
is beyond your control
(*Vera goes back to the table, sits down and refills their glasses.*)
Suicide is nobody's privilege
Suicide is a crime
He who escapes into suicide
unquestionably commits a crime
(*Vera puts a fillet of veal on Clara's plate.*)
Only man commits suicide
an animal doesn't
On the other hand
no reason exists for suicide
My dear Hoeller he said
I only hear the best about you
you do your work to our greatest satisfaction
Then we ate together
You can keep your father's house he said
the gas plant won't be built where it was planned
I have given the order
to build it in a lot
one hundred and eighty kilometers away
from your father's house
Then he jumped up quite suddenly
and said goodbye
Before I even realized what had happened
he was gone our Reichsfuehrer SS
And I had lost my appetite
so I didn't bother to sit down again
There is nothing more depressing
than ending up alone
at a table set for two
I went outside and took a walk through the camp
The air was remarkably fresh that evening
no noises nothing
As if my lungs hadn't had fresh air in months
I walked through the camp and then around the camp
and I thought about my life
I had reached a turning point a turning point
He never even had himself announced
suddenly the door flew open
and there he stood escorted of course
and said he wanted to have lunch with me
he the Reichsfuehrer SS
He'd just returned from the Fuehrer's headquarters
Roesch wasn't there

substitute commander you understand Vera
he only made that one visit to the camp
It made an impression
it certainly made an impression
(*Vera gets up, goes to the bureau and turns the music down further.*)
We had the highest possible discipline
we were a model unit
we were always ready for inspection
(*Vera turns off the music completely, takes two bottles from the bureau and sits down again.*)
We were executing a mission
for the welfare of the German people
You are executing your mission
for the welfare of the German people he said
without ever taking his eyes off me
It was impossible to escape him
there was no other choice
(*Vera opens another bottle and refills all glasses.*)
There is no way to falsify history
it can be smeared for a long time
much can be hushed up falsified
but then one day it will come to light
shining in its truest colors
that's when the smearers and the husher-uppers and the falsifiers are gone
It usually takes decades
(*Sits up and holds out his glass to Vera who refills it.*)
The devil must be exorcised by the devil
(*Empties his glass and holds it up to Vera who refills it.*)
Shame
who knew thee not
(*Gets up suddenly and lifts up his glass. Vera gets up too.*)
RUDOLF: (*With a glance at Himmler's picture on the bureau.*)
I lift up my glass
to this man
to this idea
(*To Clara.*)
And you
Of course you are unable to get up
it would only mean a desecration of this moment anyway
Nature knew
What she was doing
(*To Vera.*)
Come Vera let us drink to this idea
we shall drink to this idea
to this one idea only
(*Empties his glass. Vera drinks.*)
RUDOLF: (*With his glass held up high.*)
I feel no shame

not the least bit of shame
(Sits down again.)
My dear Vera
(Vera sits down.)
My dear kind Vera
my dearly beloved sister
we must stick together
we must be one one one
Play something
don't just sit there
play something
a nice piece of music
(Vera gets up and exits.)
If it weren't for Vera
(To Clara.)
You understand don't you
don't you understand everything
you aren't as bad as you pretend to be
not as bad as not to see
how kind my sister Vera is
(From the adjoining room Vera can be heard playing a Beethoven fantasy.)
My dear sister Vera
she always understood everything
she is the best
because of her we are alive
without her we would be gone
gone gone gone
Everything is an act of providence
an act of providence
And you aren't really all that bad
you can thank the Americans for your fate
you are our bombing victim
a living reminder
of what the Americans did to us
Millions of dead Germans millions
Munich Dresden Cologne
everything razed to the ground
You can thank the Americans for all of it
(Looks into the adjoining room.)
The Americans destroyed our culture
not only did they destroy all our cities
they also destroyed our entire culture
but you don't understand that
you'll never get that into your head
it won't fit into your stubborn leftist head
You of course enjoy the privilege of fools
otherwise we'd have already liquidated you
The privilege of fools
there are always people

who have the privilege of fools
they can do as they please
nobody takes them seriously
if one would take them seriously
one would surely have to kill them
But we aren't killing you
you're here that's all there is to it
and what it comes down to
you are our sister
the next of kin the blood relation
from the same father and mother as I and Vera
That sweet girl
You can thank God that we have her
If one day we shouldn't have her anymore
but she is the strongest of us all
the one who won't quit
how many times would I have quit already
Vera prevented it
my Vera girl my beloved Vera girl
We wouldn't have made it the two of us
we have a good sister
always had a good sister through the worst of times
you should remember this
you should remember it when you wake up
and when you go to sleep
(*With his right hand he points to the adjoining room.*)
that we owe it all to her
that we are even alive today
(*Vera has stopped playing and enters.*)
How well you played
it makes such a difference right away
Music makes everything bearable
If we make our own
A civilized nation can make its own music
Come on Vera sit down
(*Opens a bottle and pours Vera a drink.*)
I told Clara
that you saved us
you saved us
your courage
that you always held your own
in the worst of times
when I still was dwelling in the cellar
Vera my brave girl
(*Drinks.*)
We must never forget it
(*Gets up, goes to the cabinet with the guns, opens it and turns toward his sister.*)
Vera who made us possible
(*Takes out a rifle.*)

I always was a soldier
I always will be a soldier
for our cause
no matter what's coming coming coming
(*Aims the rifle at the chandelier.*)
I could shoot her down
I could knock her off gun her down
should I shoot her down
tell me Vera should I knock her off
VERA:
Rudolf please
RUDOLF:
Of course not
it would be crazy
shooting down the chandelier
(*Aims again at the chandelier.*)
But I do know how to shoot
I didn't forget
if I shoot it'll drop
right on the table
right on the table
all I have to do is pull the trigger
VERA:
You didn't forget
RUDOLF:
A soldier never forgets how to use his gun
never his gun
his gun
never
(*Puts down the rifle.*)
I only have to hold it in my hand
and I'm a soldier again
VERA:
A soldier yes
RUDOLF:
The soldier inside the soldier never dies
(*Goes to the cabinet and puts the rifle back in its place.*)
You hid it for me
you got it safely across
I owe this to you Vera
They all surrendered their weapons they threw them away
You kept my rifle for me
I feel like shooting out the window
(*Turns toward his sister.*)
but I mustn't
not yet
not yet my girl
(*Goes back to the table and sits down.*)
I could think of a few

I'd love to gun down
VERA: (*Puts a fillet of veal on his plate.*)
   You must eat something
   you just drink and you don't eat at all
   you drink so much and you don't eat at all
RUDOLF:
   Not used to it
   I am no longer used to it
   If I drink only once a year
   always on October seventh
   on Himmler's birthday
   I can't help getting drunk
   but I don't care don't care don't care
   (*To Clara.*)
   Well Clara what do you say
   I am still the same
   Von Metternich isn't it Vera Von Metternich
   the brand we drank at the camp
   That's something I always paid the greatest attention to
   that there was always enough Von Metternich at the camp
   otherwise we'd have never been able to take it
   He said my dear Hoeller
   I can depend on you
   on you and on Roesch
   he emphasized you
   not Roesch
   that coward
   Roesch really was a coward
   I never was a coward not me
VERA:
   Not you Rudolf
RUDOLF:
   That man had too much imagination
   My sense of order comes from father
   and not too much of mother's softness
VERA:
   But Rudolf you do have your tender spots from mother
RUDOLF:
   I know what Roesch is all about
   Suddenly he doesn't dare to come here anymore
   calling us
   telling us that he is sick
   I am convinced he isn't sick
   Roesch always lied
   But that also caused his downfall in the end
   I always mistrusted Roesch
   not for a moment did I trust him out of my sight
   But he can't give us away
   he'd be finished himself

Most probably he's sitting at home
warming his kneecaps at the fireplace
Roesch what a milksop
But then those are always the most unscrupulous ones
it didn't bother him at all
to send thousands and thousands into the gas
it didn't bother him at all
for me it was an effort
Vera my good girl
I am a bit worried about my retirememt
just a tiny bit
I'm afraid I might start brooding
The court distracted me
all these years I've been distracted by the court
suddenly I won't have anything to distract me
VERA:
Retirememt will be good for you
you can take walks
and do the things that you enjoy
that's what retirement is for
retirement
really Rudolf
you're not one to retire
you've always been an active man
you never get bored
We'll make our music again
you'll play the violin
I'll play the piano
Beethoven Mozart Chopin
And we'll go to the opera
now that you'll finally have the time
life will be better than ever
RUDOLF:
But maybe that's just when I won't have any peace
VERA:
It'll pass with time Rudolf
everything has always passed with time
(*Pats his hand.*)
It's there to enjoy
old age
RUDOLF:
Maybe
VERA: (*Sits down in a way she can easily turn the pages in the album and turns a page.*)
Look here our happy Rudolf
who is proud of himself
Rudolf our ideal
Where was this now
RUDOLF:
In Cracow

in front of the Sukenitza
in front of the market
VERA:
Are those Poles behind you
RUDOLF:
Yes Poles
they looked on and they laughed
How they laughed when this picture was taken
well it was a beautiful day
VERA: (*Turns a page.*)
That looks like a big hangover to me
RUDOLF:
That's when we drank to the surrender of Paris
VERA:
Where father always wanted to take mother
Have you ever been to Paris
RUDOLF
I never managed
VERA:
I never understood
why everyone gets so excited by Paris
(*Turns a page.*)
RUDOLF:
That's when I got a new uniform made
by a tailor in Litzmannstadt
VERA:
Sturmbannfuehrer Hoeller
RUDOLF:
Shortly after that
I became Obersturmbannfuehrer
VERA:
Didn't you conduct
your fist trials in Litzmannstadt
RUDOLF:
Yes of course
that's why I was there
The youngest judge on the entire Eastern front
VERA: (*Turns a page.*)
Awful
those faces
utter decay
RUDOLF:
That's a snapshot of the Jews
they sent us from Hungary
VERA:
And they were put into the labor camp
RUDOLF:
Yes and no
only those who were fit enough of course

not the others
The Jews of Hungary were a tricky case
we couldn't really use them
VERA: (*Turns a page.*)
Bruges right
RUDOLF:
That's when we made a trip to the Ardennes
and went to Bruges
and to Brussels
you see that's where we lived
I marked it with an arrow
That was some hotel
Deluxe
they cleared the entire first floor for us
we drank champagne day and night
real champagne
the Belgians were decent people
VERA:
Was that when you took a course in Law
RUDOLF:
Yes
VERA: (*Turns a page.*)
And this is me
all dressed in white
it must have been a Sunday
when we were always dressed in white
Where was Clara at that time
(*To Clara.*)
I know you were in boarding school
our brain child
the beautiful hair you had then
that's when I learned English
that's when we had a tutor from Holland
a nice man
Whatever happened to him
RUDOLF: (*Turns a page.*)
There you see nothing but Ukranians
We took care of them quickly
traitors all of them nothing but traitors
VERA:
They really look dangerous
RUDOLF: (*Pointing to it.*)
That was the exucution
Those three I shot myself
There was no one else around
That was the first time
I shot people
(*Turns a page.*)
There we were in an old villa

at the outskirts of Leningrad
it was an excursion we made in forty two
I took the picture myself
from there you could see way into the Inner City
VERA:
Who is that at the window
RUDOLF:
A medical assistant
a woman from Austria from Graz
she was shot later
because she protected some Jews
VERA: (*Turns a page.*)
A jolly group
RUDOLF:
We went skiing in Zakopane
for a whole week
we had Russian caviar
but I caught a cold
(*Vera turns a page.*)
The Fuehrer
I took it myself
with a flash bulb
as he passed
that's why he's so blurred
my only snapshot of the Fuehrer
He made an inspection in Kattowitz
that's Himmler next to him
you can't recognize him but it's him
the Silesians were cowards
traitors bastards all of them
(*Vera turns a page.*)
It was a dangerous atmosphere
You could trust no one
not even your own people
VERA: (*Turning a page.*)
Berlin Kurfuerstendamm
RUDOLF:
Yes I with Roesch
shortly before he was wounded
If I hadn't been there
he wouldn't have made it
he would have bled to death
VERA:
And he saved your life
RUDOLF:
We made a very good team
(*Empties his glass and Vera refills it.*)

But even Roesch could not be trusted
(*Vera turns a page.*)
RUDOLF:
These were the shelters
the Ukranians built before Radom
(*Vera turns a page.*)
RUDOLF:
The Dutch Circus
which we saw in Luettich
a terrific shot isn't it
(*Vera gets up and goes with the open album to Clara, showing her the picture.*)
VERA:
There you are
that's you there in the back
sitting next to Rudolf who's laughing his head off
CLARA:
Yes
VERA: (*Goes back, sits down and turns a page.*)
How old were you then
you really don't look well at all
RUDOLF:
That was in Schitomir
that's when I had bronchitis
VERA: (*Looks Rudolf in the face and then back into the album.*)
Your face looks entirely different here
as if it were someone else
RUDOLF:
I don't even know
who took the picture
maybe it was Roesch
but he wasn't in Schitomir then
he was in Danzig at that time
Who could have made it
maybe Dejaco
VERA:
The one who poisoned his seven children
RUDOLF:
He went to his death with all of them
VERA: (*Turns a page.*)
Father
His only picture in uniform
He always had an aversion
to being photographed
And mother
in her dirndl
that was in Schwaz in Tyrol
She was angry with father

RUDOLF:
    Sometimes I wonder
    if it wasn't the right time she killed herself
    She didn't live to go through
    (*Drinks.*)
    Clara all naked
    Clara our little nudie
    at the brook
VERA:
    Father in the back can you see
    he caught some fish what do you call them
RUDOLF:
    Miller's thumbs
    the same Miller's thumbs we caught as boys
VERA:
    What a shy child
    (*To Clara.*)
    Don't you want to see this picture
    You really are stark naked here
    so free and open as never again
    (*Turns a page.*)
    At Count Uiberacker's estate
    We used to go there as children
    The only place where father could really relax
    Poor Countess
    she shot herself
    when the Americans came
    Do you remember
    how she accused you
    of pushing her nephew into the pond
    You Rudolf of all people oh God
    you pushing the Countess's nephew into the pond
RUDOLF:
    He jumped all by himself
    and then he said
    I pushed him
VERA:
    After that we weren't allowed to come anymore
    we never saw those aristocrats again
RUDOLF:
    He
    the count
    he was a real Nazi hater
    she denounced her brother
    for listening to enemy stations
    but nothing happened to him
    A few months Mauthausen that's all

VERA: (*Turns a page.*)
　Who are they
RUDOLF:
　That was our elite assault group
　none of them alive anymore
　(*Drinks.*)
　they drove through a forest near Litzmannstadt
　and hit a mine field
　laid by the Polacks
VERA:
　Such beautiful men
　can you understand that Rudolf
　how can one kill such beautiful men
　their poor parents
RUDOLF:
　During war you can't give in
　to feelings
　during war
　feelings don't exist
VERA: (*Turns a page.*)
　That's our President
　can you see
　what a sweet boy
　in his Hitler Youth uniform
　who's that behind him
RUDOLF:
　No idea
　(*Looks closer.*)
　I can't tell
VERA:
　There you see
　what becomes of sweet little boys
　if they're capable
　(*Turns a page.*)
RUDOLF:
　That's Roesch
VERA:
　With a Polish woman
RUDOLF:
　Well naturally
　there were no others
VERA:
　What gorgeous black hair that woman had
RUDOLF:
　That one was from Warsaw
　she was gassed right away
　(*Vera turns a page.*)
　That's Auschwitz

That's when we visited Hoess
Himmler was to be there too
but then he didn't come
Back there was the ramp
that's where the trains came in
that's where they drove them through
VERA:
Terrible
RUDOLF
During war you can't have any feelings
and you actually don't have them
VERA:
Luckily you weren't in Auschwitz
RUDOLF:
It wasn't meant to be
(*Points at the picture.*)
That's where they drove them in
and that's where they were gassed
VERA:
How many were actually gassed in Auschwitz
RUDOLF:
Two and a half million
that's what Eichmann said
VERA:
Two and a half million
RUDOLF:
That's what Eichmann said to Gluecks
VERA: (*Turns a page.*)
I'm glad you weren't in Auschwitz
I don't know but I'm glad
Where you were
that was different altogether
And here's Ludwig our uncle Ludwig
when he took the apprentice's final exam
He was so proud of you
you in your uniform next to him
What a pity he had to die
That's when we always got such excellent meat
and those delicious sausages
(*Turns a page.*)
That's the Academy concert
and you in the first row
RUDOLF:
And you next to me
VERA:
We got the tickets from Roesch
didn't we
Yes because his daughter passed the academy exam
Beethoven's Fifth remember

And that's Elli Ney sitting there
(*Turns a page.*)
How good these pictures are
don't you think
if one looks at them only once a year
and doesn't expose them to light
Schwarzbach
Reichenall
Piding
we were happy then weren't we Rudolf
oh come on I have to give you a kiss
(*Moves closer to Rudolf and kisses him on the forehead.*)
Nobody can take these memories away from us
our memories
We can't lose them
(*Turns a page.*)
Father always said that too
The Valley of Roses
I never saw it again
Maria Saal the church
there you stand with the flowers
you picked for me
(*Turns a page.*)
Oh that's when you were wounded
but I was proud of you
everybody admired me
because you were wounded
I went through town with my head up high
and I could feel
how they admired me
because you were wounded
luckily nothing serious
(*Turns a page.*)
Berlin after the first attack
(*To Rudolf.*)
Did you take this picture
Is that one dead

RUDOLF:
Yes and behind him another one see

VERA:
Terrible
(*Turns a page.*)
That's when our parents took Clara out of boarding school
and sent her to Tyrol
(*To Clara.*)
To Reverend Langthaler
Why are you so quiet
instead of enjoying these pictures
You'd love to ruin our evening

(*Turns a page.*)
The Giant Mountains
In Alsace you wrote underneath
What a lovely handwriting you had
to this day your handwriting is beautiful
(*Turns a page.*)
Verdun
(*After a pause.*)
Oh Rudolf that we have to hide
and look at this so secretly
that's really terrible
And yet the majority thinks just like us
the majority hides that's what's so terrible
it's really absurd
The majority thinks like us and must do so secretly
Even if they insist on the contrary
they still are National Socialists all of them
it's written all over their faces
but they don't admit it
I don't know anyone who doesn't think like us
Except for the doctor and a few others
but they are too few to count
That is the horror Rudolf
that we don't show the world who we are
we don't show it
instead of showing it quite openly
just showing it

RUDOLF:
Just wait and see
the time will come for us to show it again
Everything indicates that we will show it again
and not only show it

VERA:
Then again we do have a President now
who was a National Socialist

RUDOLF:
There you are
this is proof of how far we've already come
no need to worry
don't you worry Vera
everything is going our way
it is no longer a question of waiting
and furthermore don't we have a whole bunch
of other leading politicians
who were National Socialists

VERA: (*Closes the album.*)
Yes that is true
(*To Clara.*)
We will be back in power soon

Then the likes of you won't have a chance
Just like you all these crazies ran amok
undermining our country violating its ideals
I'm really angry with you
sitting here silently all evening
but you won't manage to ruin our evening
And Rudolf really controlled himself
Last year he forced you to put on
the concentration camp jacket not today
And I had to shave your head last year remember
he kept referring to you as a camp inmate
he didn't do it today
Spoil sport
(*Opens the album again, looks through it.*)
Freiburg in Breisgau
we still saw it before they wrecked it
those Americans
(*Turns a page.*)
Wuerzburg
All those beautiful cities they completely ruined them for us
Those Americans
(*Closes the album.*)
Good God how beautiful Germany once was
(*Rudolf has tried for a while to pull the pistol from his belt, he's just succeeded and is flaunting it now in Vera's face.*)
VERA: (*Frightened.*)
Rudolf please
I ask you please
RUDOLF:
I could blast you down if I wanted to
I could blast them all
I'm out of practice of course
but I could blast you all just like you are
(*Gets up.*)
VERA:
Rudolf please
you drank too much
RUDOLF:
If I feel like it
I can blow your guts out
(*Vera jumps up.*)
RUDOLF:
Back to your seat
that's an order
back to your seat
(*Vera sits down again.*)
RUDOLF:
Let me tell you
if I wanted to I'd blast you away

VERA:
   Rudolf that's going too far
RUDOLF:
   I decide
   what's going too far
VERA:
   If anyone hears you
   (*Looks to the windows.*)
RUDOLF:
   There's no one to hear me
   nobody can hear me
   if I just felt like it
   (*Goes to Clara and puts the pistol to her neck. After a pause.*)
   But I don't feel like it
   and the pistol isn't even loaded
   (*Proves it with one motion of his hand.*)
   There are no bullets in this pistol
VERA:
   You're pushing your luck
   Rudolf
   please
RUDOLF:
   It always comes down to
   whether one does it or does not
   it's not a question of character
   (*Sits down and puts the pistol on the table.*)
VERA:
   You're drunk Rudolf
   (*Reproachfully to both.*)
   Because you didn't eat my delicious dinner
   you ate nothing
   (*To Clara.*)
   You didn't touch anything
   (*To Rudolf.*)
   and neither did you
   (*To Rudolf referring to Clara.*)
   How she hates us
   do you see how she hates us
   (*Rudolf takes his glass and empties it.*)
VERA:
   Rudolf I beg you
RUDOLF:
   You can't tell me what to do
   not even you
   nobody
   (*Takes the pistol and points it around wildly.*)
   I give you one more chance

one more chance is all I give you
one more chance
(*Holds his chest and falls over onto the table.*)
VERA: (*Has jumped up and exclaims pathetically.*)
Oh my God
(*She rushes to him and takes his pulse.*)
He's had an attack
Clara an attack
His heart Clara
his heart
(*Gets up and goes to the doors and windows, turns Beethoven's Fifth back on exactly where it was interrupted before.
Comes back to the table.*)
Now what
what do we do now
(*Drags Rudolf from the chair and tries to pull him over to the sofa; she succeeds. Rudolf appears to be conscious, but he can't articulate anymore, he can only groan.*)
VERA: (*Kneels down in front of him.*)
Rudolf
can you hear me Rudolf
my dear Rudolf
my sweet dear Rudolf
(*Starts to take off his SS uniform.*)
Terrible just terrible
(*To Clara.*)
What are you sitting there staring at me
how terrible
(*Takes off his jacket.*)
That it had to come to this
Such a beautiful day
(*Pulls off his boots and tries to take off his trousers as Clara is watching her.*)
It's a tragedy
a tragedy
(*Grabs the uniform pieces, runs out with them, returns immediately to remove Himmler's picture. On her way out she remembers the pistol, which lies on the table; takes the pistol, leaves and returns immediately. She tries to put her brother in his civilian jacket.
Bends over Rudolf, kisses him, then to Clara:*)
It's your fault
you and your silence
you and your endless silence
(*Goes to the telephone and calls the doctor. Lights fade. As the curtain is coming down:*)
Doctor Fromm please

Curtain.

THE PRESIDENT
(Württembergische Staatstheater Stuttgart; Dir.: Claus Peymann)

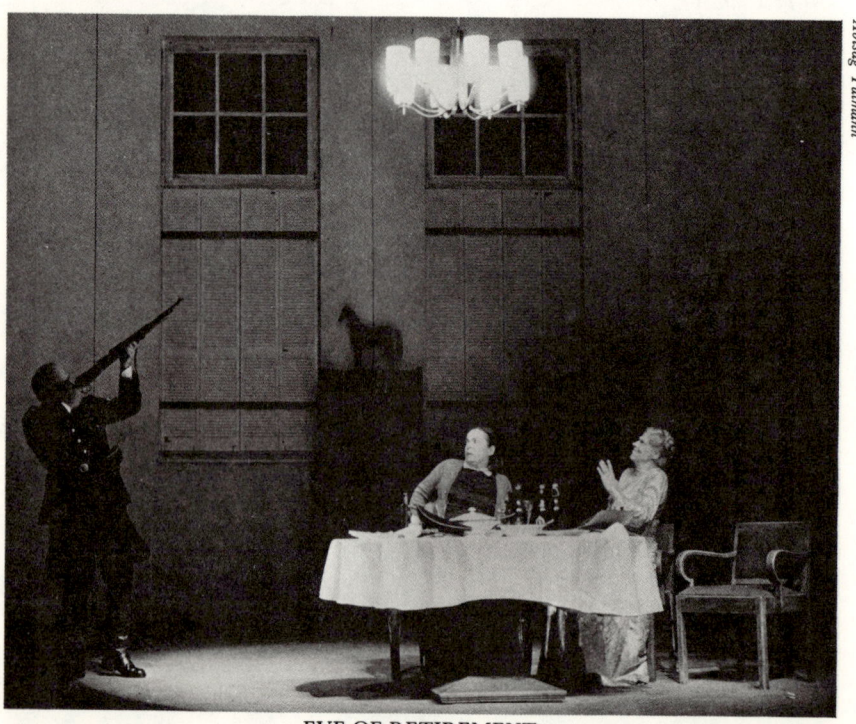

EVE OF RETIREMENT
(Württembergische Staatstheater Stuttgart; Dir.: Claus Peymann)

Selections from Thomas Bernhard

IS IT A COMEDY? IS IT A TRAGEDY?

Yesterday, after not having been to the theatre in weeks, I wanted to go to the theatre, but even two hours before curtain time, while working on my science papers, hence still in my room, the thought occurred to me and I couldn't tell whether on top or in the back of my mind cluttered as it was with all that medical stuff, which I would finally have to finish for the sake not so much of my parents but of my own over-exerted head, that I'd better stay away from the theatre.

I haven't been to the theatre in eight, maybe ten, weeks, I said to myself, and I know very well why I stopped going to the theatre, I despise the theatre, I hate actors, theatre is an outrageous insult, an insulting outrage, and now, all of a sudden, I am off to the theatre again? What's that all about?

You know that the theatre is an obscenity, you are even going to write a piece on theatre, you've got it all in your head, a piece on theatre to deal the theatre its death blow! All about the theatre, what theatre *is*, what actors *are*, all about playwrights, producers, etc.

There I was, more and more obsessed with theatre, less and less concerned about pathology, a failure in my attempt to ignore the theatre, in my effort to advance pathology. A failure! A failure!

I got dressed and went out.

It only takes me half an hour to walk to the theatre. In this half hour it became quite clear to me that I could *not* go to the theatre, that I *was* barred, once and for all, from all theatres, all performances.

Once you're finished with your piece, I thought, it will be time, it will be all right for you to go to the theatre again, if only to find out that your thesis is *right*.

Now I was embarrassed that I had let it come to this, that I had actually bought myself a ticket—the ticket was *paid* for *by*, not *given to* me—and that I had been torturing myself for two days in the belief that I would be going to the theatre to watch a performance, to see actors and smell behind all those actors a dreadful, an absolutely lousy director (Mr. T.H.!) etc. . . . and, worst of all, that I had changed my clothes for the theatre. You actually *changed your clothes* for the theatre, I thought.

My piece on theatre, some day, my piece on theatre! One describes well what one hates, I thought. With its five, possibly seven, sections entitled THEATRE-THEATRE? my study should be finished in no time at all. (Once finished, I'll burn it, because it would make no sense publishing it, you just read through it and burn it. Publishing it would be ridiculous, *a purpose defeated*!) First section THE PERFORMERS, second section THE PERFORMERS INSIDE THE PERFORMERS, third section THE PERFORMERS INSIDE THE PERFORMERS OF THE PERFORMERS, etc. . . . fourth section THEATRICAL EXCESSES, etc. . . . last section SO, WHAT IS THEATRE?

With these thoughts I got as far as the Volksgarten.*

I sit down on a bench near the tavern, even though sitting down on a park bench can be fatal at this time of year and I watch, intensely, with great pleasure, with the utmost concentration, *who* is entering the theatre and *how*.

It gives me tremendous pleasure *not* to enter.

But you ought to go there, I think, if for no other reason but to show some concern for your poverty by selling the ticket, *go there*, I say to myself and while I am thinking this, it gives me great satisfaction to rub the ticket between my right thumb and index finger, rubbing away the theatre.

At first, I say to myself, more and more people keep entering the theatre, then less and less. Finally, no one enters the theatre.

The performance has started I think as I get up to head in the direction of the inner city, I am freezing, I had nothing to eat and, it just occurs to me, no one to talk to in over a week, when suddenly I am being talked to: a man has approached me, I hear the man ask what time it is and I hear myself yell: "Eight o'clock." "It's eight o'clock," I say, "the performance has started."

Now I turn around and I see the man.

The man is tall and skinny.

Besides that man there is no one in the park, I think.

And immediately I think that I have nothing to lose.

But to actually say the words *"I have nothing to lose!"* to say them out loud seems stupid to me, so I don't say anything, although I am much tempted to.

He had lost his watch, the man said.

"Since I've lost my watch, I am forced, from time to time, to walk up to people and talk to them."

He laughed.

"If I hadn't lost my watch, I wouldn't have talked to you," he said, "I would have talked to *nobody*."

He'd find it most interesting, the man said, that now, after I told him that it was eight o'clock, he'd know that it *is* eight o'clock and that this very

---

*The park next to the Vienna Burgtheater.

day he had been walking continuously for eight hours, "without a break," he said—in pursuit of one thought only, "not back and forth," he said, but always "straight ahead, yet, as I can see now, always in a circle. Crazy, isn't it?"

I saw that the man was wearing women's pumps and the man saw that I had seen he was wearing women's pumps.

"Yes," he said, "now you might have something to think about."

"I wanted to go to the theatre," I said quickly to distract the man and myself from the pumps, "but right in front of the theatre I turned around and didn't go in."

"I've been in that theatre many times," the man said, he had introduced himself, but I forgot his name immediately, I never remember names, "and then, one day, it was for the last time, just as everyone, one day, has been to the theatre for the last time, don't laugh," said the man, "once everything happens for the last time, don't laugh!"

"Oh," he said, "what's playing today? No, no," he said quickly, "don't tell me what's playing today. . . ."

He'd been coming to this park every day, the man said, "since the beginning of the theatre season I'd always walk around this corner, because from here, from this corner, you see, from the tavern corner, I can watch the theatre-goers. Strange people," he said.

"Of course one should know what's playing today," he said, "but don't *you* tell me what's playing today. To me it's most interesting, for once *not* to know what's playing. Is it a comedy? Is it a tragedy?" he said and added immediately, "nono, don't tell me *what* it is. Don't tell me!"

The man is fifty, or fifty-five, I think.

He suggests that we walk in the direction of the parliament.

"Let's walk to the parliament," he said "and back again. There's always such a strange hush once the performance has started, I *love* the theatre. . . ."

He walked very quickly and it was almost unbearable for me to watch him move, the thought of him wearing women's pumps made me nauseous.

"Every day I take the same number of steps on this route, that is to say," he said, "that in these shoes it takes me exactly three hundred and twenty-eight steps to get from the tavern to the parliament, up to the fence. In the buckled shoes it takes me exactly three hundred and ten. And to the Swiss wing—he meant the Swiss wing of the Imperial Palace—four hundred and fourteen steps in these shoes, three hundred and twenty nine in the buckled shoes! Women's pumps, you might think and you might find it repulsive, I know," said the man.

"But I only go out in the dark. My coming to this park every evening, always at the same time, always half an hour before curtain time, is due, as you can imagine, to an emotional shock. This emotional shock dates back more than twenty years and it is closely related to those women's pumps. An incident," he said, "An incident. The atmosphere now is exactly the same as it was then: In the theatre, the curtain's just gone up, the actors are beginning to play, not a soul out here in the streets . . . Now," said the man, as we got back to the tavern again, "let's go to the Swiss wing."

A lunatic? I thought as we were walking to the Swiss wing, side by side. The man said: "This world is an out and out legalistic world, as you may not know. This world is one bloody legalism. The world is a penitentiary!"

He said: "It's been exactly forty-eight days since I last met a man here in this park at the exact same time. I asked *that* man too what time it was. That man too told me that it was eight o'clock. Oddly enough, I'm always asking at eight o'clock what time it is. That man too walked with me to the parliament and from there to the Swiss wing. Incidentally," said the man, "I did not, and that's the truth, lose my watch, I don't lose my watch. My watch, you see, is right here," he said and held his wrist up to my face so that I could see his watch.

"A trick," he said, "but to continue: this man, whom I met forty-eight days ago, was a young man your age. Quiet, just like you, *un*decided at first, just like you, then ready to come with me. A science student," the man said, "I told *him* too that an emotional shock, an incident dating back a long time was the reason for my coming to this park every evening. In women's pumps. Identical reactions," said the man and:

"Incidentally, I've never seen a policeman here. For the last few days the police has been avoiding the Volksgarten to focus on the City Park instead, and I know why. . . ."

"Now it would indeed be interesting to know," he said, "if at this very moment, as we are walking to the Swiss wing, they are playing a comedy or a tragedy. . . . This is the first time I don't know what's playing. But you mustn't tell me. . . . No, don't tell me! If I keep studying you, if I concentrate on nothing but you I should have no trouble figuring out whether they are playing a tragedy or a comedy right now. Yes," he said, "in time my observations of your personage would lead me to find out everything that's going on inside the theatre, everything that's going on outside the theatre, everything about the world, since this has everything to do with you. In the process of studying you with the greatest intensity I might actually reach the point where I know everything about you. . . ."

As we reached the facade of the Swiss wing, he said, "Right here, the young man, whom I met forty-eight days ago, took his leave. You want to know *how*? Be careful! Ah!" he said, "so you're *not* taking your leave? You're *not* saying Good Night to me? Well then," he said, "let's go back to where we came from. And where did we come from? Oh yes, from the tavern. What's so odd about people is how they constantly confuse themselves with others! So," he said, "you wanted to see tonight's performance. Although you hate the theatre, as you say. *Hate* the theatre, I love it. . . ."

Now I realized that the man also had a woman's hat on his head. The coat he was wearing was also a woman's coat, a woman's winter coat.

In fact, he was wearing nothing but women's clothes, I thought.

"During the summer," he said, "I don't come to this park, nothing's playing in the theatre then either, but *when* they are playing, I come to this park, then—when they are playing—no one but me comes to this park, because it's much too cold then in this park. Occasionally, a young man would come through this park and I'd approach him immediately, as you know, asking him to come with me, once to the parliament and once to the Swiss wing, then always back again. . . ."

"But no one, and I find this noteworthy," he said, "has yet walked with me *twice* to the parliament and *twice* to the Swiss wing, thus *four times* back to the tavern. Now, we've walked *twice* to the parliament and *twice* to the Swiss wing and back again," he said, "that's enough. If you like to," he said, "why don't you accompany me on my way home. No one has ever accompanied me from here on my way home."

He lived in the twentieth district.

He was *lodging* in the apartment of his parents, who had died ("Suicide, young man, suicide!") six weeks ago.

"We have to cross the Danube," he said.

The man interested me and I wanted to accompany him as far as possible.

"When we reach the Danube, you must turn back," he said, "You must not come with me further than the Danube. When we get to the Danube, don't ask me *why*!"

Behind the army quarters, a hundred meters away from the bridge leading to the twentieth district, the man stopped all of a sudden, looked down to the water and said: "Here, this is the spot."

He turned toward me and repeated: "This is the spot."

And he said: "I pushed her off very quickly. The clothes I am wearing are her clothes."

Then he signaled me, which meant *Go!*

He wanted to be alone.

"*Leave!*" he commanded.

I didn't leave right away.

I let him speak. "Twenty two years and eight months ago," he said.

"And if you believe that prisons are fun, you are wrong! The whole world is one bloody legalism. And tonight, let me tell you, in that theatre over there, believe it or not, they are playing a comedy, *yes indeed,* a comedy."

AN ACTOR*

An actor performs in a fairy tale, in which he plays the part of the wicked wizard . . . they throw a sheep skin over him, stick him in a pair of shoes, which are much too short for him and squeeze his feet . . . *but nobody can see that* . . . he loves playing for children *so* much, because they are his *best audiences* . . . *Naturally,* the children, three hundred, get scared when he enters, because they are thoroughly enthralled by the young lovers, on whom the wizard casts his magic spell, transforming them into two animals (*creeping mammals*) . . . They would be happiest watching only the young lovers, but this is a good play, a good fairy tale . . . and a real, a good fairy tale (play) must feature one character who is evil (evil minded), opaque, who has to (sets out to) destroy or at least ridicule that which is good, transparent. Since the curtain is now rising for the second time (and the play is taking its course), the children can no longer be constrained, they jump out of their seats and up onto the stage and there seem to be not just three hundred, but thousands, millions of them . . . and although the actor as the wizard, behind his wizard's mask, is crying, imploring them to stop hitting and kicking him, they won't listen, but keep hitting him (with sharp, pointed objects, scissors and knives) until he stops moving, until he *is dead* . . . as soon as the other actors, who had been standing backstage, waiting for their entrances without noticing the tragedy in the fairy tale play, come rushing out and realize that their fellow actor, the best of them, the wizard, the actor playing the wizard is dead, the children who killed him burst into a monstrous fit of laughter, an outburst so great that they all lose their minds *in it.*

---

*From Bernhard's novel *Amras*.